"Finley and Henderson convey an important message that all Americans can make civil discourse a reality by providing us with the tools and examples needed to make it happen. This book should be required reading in high schools and universities."

—Michael Benedict, author of *The Civil Society Playbook: A Commonsense Plan for a Return to Civility*

"In a clear and engaging way, Nolan, Stephen, and Lynne explain the need for and how to accomplish civility. Greater civility is a *must* for a brighter future in our society. This is not just a book to be read but a book to be lived."

—Rick Snyder, 48th governor of Michigan

"Nolan Finley and Stephen Henderson have written an essential book for our times: a story of an unlikely friendship across partisan divides and, even more, a guide to learning and growing together even when we disagree. Civility and civic engagement are critical for our democracy."

—Santa J. Ono, president, University of Michigan

"Civility is not dead! But it's bloodied, beaten, and mortally wounded. The arena of American politics has descended into racism, sexism, and xenophobia. Finger-pointing and name-calling have become our weapons. The chief motivation is to win, not to find answers to our common problems.

This book gives us a pathway to reach what Abraham Lincoln called 'the better angels of our nature.' For years, Stephen Henderson and Nolan Finley have engaged in passionate debates over policy and politics, yet they have consistently refused to demonize each other. They are articulate examples of how to prioritize collaboration over conflict, dialogue over dismissal.

If you're looking for justification to stand in your ideological corner and shout at your opponent, this book is not for you. But if you're looking for a way to bridge the deep divisions that continue to separate us, I urge you to read, study, and open yourself to the real-life solutions you'll find in these pages."

—Huel Perkins, Emmy award–winning news anchor, WJBK-TV from 1989–2022

"Two veteran journalists from opposing ends of the political spectrum show us that meaningful dialogue across ideological divides isn't just possible—it's transformative. Through their groundbreaking work with the Civility Project and this practical guide, Nolan Finley and Stephen Henderson give us concrete tools to move beyond toxic polarization toward more productive conversations that strengthen the fabric of our society."

—Bridget McCormack, president and CEO, American Arbitration Association

"Too many people write off those who don't share the 'right' views, preferring to live in their own echo chambers. In this artful and lively book, Nolan Finley and Stephen Henderson offer a guide, rooted in their own unlikely friendship, to how we can bridge political divides and find our shared humanity. Bravo."

—Ingrid Jacques, national opinion columnist, *USA Today*

"At a critical time in our nation's history, Nolan Finley and Stephen Henderson show us the path toward civil and constructive political discourse. I know firsthand of the impact of the Civility Project to draw us away from reactionary attitudes and reductionist rationalizations. Nolan and Stephen challenge us to find common ground on a human level, one conversation at a time. Together, they renew our faith in democracy and in one another."

—Ora Hirsch Pescovitz, president, Oakland University

"Nolan and Stephen are like the old cartoon characters, Ralph Wolf and Sam Sheepdog. They pummel each other from nine to five, then punch out at the time clock and walk home with their lunch pails and their arms around each other. Please try it."

—Devin Scillian, news anchor, WDIV-TV from 1995–2024

# THE
# Civility
# BOOK

# THE
# Civility
# BOOK

A GUIDE TO BUILDING BRIDGES ACROSS THE POLITICAL DIVIDE

**NOLAN FINLEY & STEPHEN HENDERSON**
with Lynne Golodner

Wayne State University Press
Detroit, Michigan

© 2025 by Nolan Finley, Lynne Golodner, and Stephen Henderson. All rights reserved. No part of this book may be reproduced without formal permission.

ISBN 9780814352182 (paperback)
ISBN 9780814352199 (ebook)

Library of Congress Control Number: 2024952867

Cover design by Will Brown.

Wayne State University Press rests on Waawiyaataanong, also referred to as Detroit, the ancestral and contemporary homeland of the Three Fires Confederacy. These sovereign lands were granted by the Ojibwe, Odawa, Potawatomi, and Wyandot Nations, in 1807, through the Treaty of Detroit. Wayne State University Press affirms Indigenous sovereignty and honors all tribes with a connection to Detroit. With our Native neighbors, the press works to advance educational equity and promote a better future for the earth and all people.

Wayne State University Press
Leonard N. Simons Building
4809 Woodward Avenue
Detroit, Michigan 48201-1309

Visit us online at wsupress.wayne.edu.

*To all our children and grandchildren,
to whom we hope to leave a more civil world*

# Contents

| | | |
|---|---|---|
| | Foreword by Debbie Dingell and Fred Upton | xi |
| | Introduction | 1 |
| 1. | What Civility Is and Why It Matters | 19 |
| 2. | The Causes and Effects of Incivility | 29 |
| 3. | The Four Pillars of Civility | 53 |
| 4. | Pillar 1: Dropping Assumptions | 63 |
| 5. | Pillar 2: Setting Honest Goals | 73 |
| 6. | Pillar 3: Practicing Active Listening | 81 |
| 7. | Pillar 4: Keep Coming Back | 87 |
| 8. | Civility in Community | 93 |
| 9. | Acting Where You Have Agency | 99 |
| | Conclusion: Civility in Action | 107 |
| | Meet the People behind the Civility Project | 111 |
| | Acknowledgments | 125 |
| | Appendix I: A Civility Curriculum | 127 |
| | Appendix II: Civility Resources | 133 |
| | Letters from Civility Sponsors | 161 |

# Foreword

Debbie Dingell and Fred Upton say they don't know two members of Congress who are closer than they are. A Republican, Fred was the representative from Michigan's 6th congressional district from 1987 until 2023. A Democrat, Debbie Dingell represented the 12th congressional district of Michigan (now the 6th) since 2015, succeeding her husband, John Dingell, the revered longest-serving member of Congress in US history. John Dingell passed away in 2019. Fred and John were longtime friends and colleagues, and along with Fred's wife, Amey Rulon-Miller, the couples have been friends for decades.

Fred and Debbie's bipartisan friendship and working relationship has been a model for Nolan Finley and Stephen Henderson, which is why they were eager to have the two representatives introduce this book. Fred and Debbie have been involved in the Great Lakes Civility Project in various ways and continue to be supportive of it.

"I don't think two members of Congress could be closer than Debbie and me," said Fred. "We used to talk every day. Now, we talk a couple times a week. We go back 35 years. We were good friends when she was a spouse. John Dingell was the most respected member of Congress, the dean of the House, and one of my best buddies. Our offices were across the hall from each other, so we really got to know each other well. We literally would walk to vote together for years."

The foundation for their friendship was Michigan, Fred said: "Our love for the Great Lakes, knowing that we're the auto state, I was cochair of the Auto Caucus with a number of members of the largest bipartisan caucus on the Hill. Even though I don't have an auto-assembly facility in my district, we have a lot of auto parts, and [auto parts providers/companies are] critical to Michigan's economy."

Two keys to their friendship are honesty and humor. Fred would often find himself on the Democratic side of the House of Representatives, rounding up votes for whatever cause he was supporting, and he'd sit on the arm of the chair and play little videos, and the pair and other colleagues would crack up. "That was the same relationship that I had with Big John," Fred said.

"There are a lot of interests that put us together," Fred added. "And our delegation was one of the strongest in the country. Between our committee chairs, the seniority that we had on both sides of the aisle. It's not the same today, tragically. It just isn't. But Debbie was part of the glue that made things work."

They even held bipartisan fundraisers together in their home districts, and people came with two checks, one for each of them, Fred recalled.

"We both met visitors at the door. We were not ashamed to be seen or work together on any issue. When we disagree—and we do—we're agreeable, and we respect each other; we understand where we each come from," Fred said. "I think the world of Debbie and the work that she does."

Fred retired from Congress on January 3, 2023, but he had to be out of his office in Washington, DC, in early December. So Debbie invited him to set up in her office. He set a picture of his family on a little table and appreciated the Michigan football helmet she displayed, so he didn't have to bring his own. She gave him a key to the office, and he brought his coffee machine.

"Fred's been my dearest friend forever and was John's dearest friend," Debbie echoed. "Fred's the one that told John to get on the Energy and Commerce Committee. We shared the ups and downs of life, and we have more things in common than differences. We talk about what different people think about the issues, searching for the common ground."

Together, they try to look at issues from all perspectives, Debbie said. "*Compromise* isn't a dirty word. We're more concerned with how we solve the problem. We're not interested in credit; we're interested in solving the problem."

To get things done, they say, you must work on both sides of the aisle but also have trust and friendship.

"Without that trust, you're doomed," Fred said. "Today's chaotic, toxic, partisan climate is why they can't get things done."

The pair support the Great Lakes Civility Project because "it's not just in government that we're losing civility," Debbie said. "In everything we do, it's becoming easier and easier to not show respect for people, to say things that are harsh and unkind, and to not believe truths. Civility matters. And kindness and empathy and compassion.

"God gave us two ears and one mouth for a reason: to listen more and talk less," Debbie said. "Our democracy depends upon people listening to each other, understanding different perspectives, and finding common ground. I'm also worried that violence is becoming too easy and all of this disruptive behavior, this hate language and violence, are becoming normalized."

"The really outstanding thing about Steve and Nolan," said Fred, "is that they're not afraid to expose the 'gotcha' moments that sometimes confront us. They see through that, expose it, and [don't] let it move forward. They respect those that stand up to the 'gotcha,' the political crap that too many of our colleagues refuse to stamp out."

One of the hallmarks of Fred's congressional career was visiting schools. It wasn't for partisan speeches; it was just to meet his constituents. Every day, he encounters someone who remembers him from when they were children. The conversations they had as real people built bonds that are lasting a lifetime.

"They don't care if you have an *R* or a *D* next to your name," Fred said. "They just want the job done. Most people aren't cardcarrying members of the Republican or Democratic Party. They want the job done, and they can't understand this dysfunction in DC when it seems like the sweet spot can be pretty big to get some things done. Issues that plague the world.

"Today's world is the toughest I think it's ever been, maybe except for World War II," Fred said. "We have a responsibility not only to our constituents but to the rest of the world to show that we can govern and identify right and wrong and move forward so that we have a better quality of life for everyone.

"Personal relationships often drive where we are, and they shouldn't be partisan," Fred concluded.

"It's really important that people reach out to each other, get to know each other, learn from each other's different perspectives, and try to bring more people together instead of focusing on what divides us," Debbie said.

Not too long ago, Fred and Debbie were with colleagues headed to dinner. President Trump was in Fred's district in Michigan, and he said some unkind things about the late John Dingell. Fred and Debbie were driving together, and they listened to the character attack on the radio in the car. Debbie was understandably upset. The next day, Fred called the president and demanded that he call Debbie with an apology. He refused.

"I didn't want an apology," Debbie said. "I'd like for everybody to use this as a learning moment, to take a deep breath and understand that words have consequences. Let's use this as a moment to remind each other to treat each other with respect and dignity."

*Debbie Dingell and Fred Upton*

# Introduction

Like many relationships, our collaboration on the Great Lakes Civility Project got its start in a bar.

In the fall of 2011, we were assigned by our respective newspapers, *The Detroit News* and the *Detroit Free Press*, to cover the biennial state Republican Party Leadership Conference on Michigan's Mackinac Island. Roughly 1,500 rank-and-file Republicans, along with the party's leadership, donors, and future gubernatorial and presidential hopefuls, had landed on the motorless island for three days of schmoozing and boozing.

Delegates filled the aptly named Grand Hotel during the day to work through the official agenda and then spilled across Mackinac at night, cramming the streets with their red-white-and-blue get-ups and drinking free liquor at dozens of receptions and fundraisers hosted by politicians and their corporate sponsors.

It tends to get pretty drunk out in a hurry.

We were there from different newspapers but for the same reason—to add commentary to the coverage of the event. At the time, Stephen was the editorial page editor of the *Detroit Free Press*, a progressive newspaper generally aligned with the Democratic Party. Nolan held, and still does, the same role at *The Detroit News*, a conservative publication that leans toward Republicans.

By this point, we had known each other for a couple of years and were already being thrown together on television shows and public panels where audiences expected us to fight. And we did. A lot. And with a good deal of heat.

But something unlikely also happened. We developed a real friendship despite our on-air combat and obvious deep differences.

Often after a joint appearance, we'd find ourselves in a bar, talking for hours over bourbon. We should mention here that bourbon is one of our biggest common denominators. Stephen developed his taste for the whiskey while working at the *Lexington Herald-Leader*; Nolan, a native Kentuckian, was born with his.

Our intent that night was to share a glass or two and put the day behind us. We filed our columns, walked out of the makeshift pressroom in the theater of the Grand, worked our way across the world's longest hotel porch, and broke free of the crowd. We headed down the hill toward downtown in search of a suitable watering hole.

As always happens when we're together, we got a lot of curious looks and more than a few "What are you two doing together?" comments. After all, we are professional rivals and polar opposites in nearly every way.

On Main Street, we dodged the horse droppings and peered into bar after bar throbbing with loud music and crowds spilling out the doors. We finally settled on the Mustang Lounge, an old-time Mackinac establishment that typically serves as a hangout for island natives and summer workers but on that night was jammed with Republicans hell-bent on a party. We managed to find empty bar stools and settled in. A dance band was playing, but not so loud that we couldn't talk.

In a crowd that was mostly White and completely conservative, it was an uncomfortable venue for Stephen. He had recently written some columns that many Republicans thought had crossed the line in their pointed criticism of the GOP. He was getting plenty of stink eyes.

After a while, Nolan got up to use the restroom. As he crossed the dance floor, he was stopped by two middle-aged women whom he recognized as frequent letter writers to the *News*. They had recently launched a conservative website that was 100 percent dedicated to attacking President Barack Obama.

One of the women grabbed Nolan's arm and demanded, "Is that Stephen Henderson you're drinking with? How can you be friends with him? We just hate him. He's so awful."

Nolan remembers being stunned by their anger. He didn't agree with Stephen's opinions either, but he was surprised by the pair's vehemence and that they felt so personally and passionately offended by him.

"You hate him?" Nolan responded. "Do you know him? Have you ever spoken with him?"

They admitted they hadn't, adding, "But we know what he writes."

"Do me a favor," Nolan said. "My seat is empty. Go over and introduce yourself. Talk to him."

To their credit, they did just that. At first, Nolan was worried he'd set up Stephen for yet another nasty encounter in a weekend that had been full of them.

But watching from the other side of the room, the women, while animated, appeared to be engaging Stephen in polite conversation. And for his part, Stephen was letting them talk and was asking them questions.

As it turned out, the two conservative women had a substantive beef with him. This encounter happened as the massive auto bankruptcies (General Motors and Chrysler, with Ford selling everything but its nameplate to avoid forced reorganization) were wrapping up, and the consequences of the economic carnage were being realized.

As part of the efforts to save the automotive companies, a sprawling network of car dealers that had supported major pillars of the American economy was being shredded. Chrysler announced in 2009 that it would close nearly 800 dealerships, a quarter of its total. General Motors closed more than 2,000. One of the conservative women who "hated" Stephen was part of a family that owned dealerships in Michigan and stood to be devastated by the planned closures.

At the bar on Mackinac, that's where the conversation began. Stephen had been writing in favor of the bankruptcies as a way to preserve the industry and the money it pumped into Michigan. He had argued that the structured reorganizations, as painful as they might be, were a far better outcome than an unmanaged fire sale at any of the auto companies.

He also strongly supported the administration of President Obama, which had intervened in the bankruptcy court proceedings and reordered the priority for creditors. Pensions would be largely preserved under the Obama plans, and wealthier creditors would be asked to make bigger sacrifices—along with owners of dealerships, some of whom were just being jettisoned.

The conservative women explained that their livelihoods were on the line, and they found Stephen's exuberance for the bankruptcies to be dismissive of them and callous. Stephen listened. He asked lots of questions about their work and their businesses. He wanted to know what they'd do if their dealerships closed and what effect it would have on their families. They told Stephen that the rule-breaking interference of the Obama administration was adding insult to injury. The expectations about fairness and due process were being tossed aside.

Stephen then explained that despite what he understood about their individual challenges, he still believed the bankruptcies were the best thing for the industry, for the national economy, and especially for Detroit and the state of Michigan. The alternative was unthinkable and would lead to widespread turmoil that could bankrupt dealerships anyway, along with lots of other institutions and sectors.

They talked for 20 minutes. Then 40. Then an hour, and an hour and a half. They listened to each other, acknowledged seeing each other's points, but never backed away from the core of what they were saying or what they believed.

Finally, tired of watching the ice in his drink melt, Nolan walked over and coaxed the two women away from Stephen. As they were moving toward the door, he asked them how it went.

"He's so wonderful!" one of the ladies gushed. "We just love him."

Now, in 90 minutes, nothing about the women or their grievances had changed. Nothing about Stephen or his opinions had changed. What had happened was they had taken the time to talk—and more importantly, to listen. While still disagreeing, they walked away with a greater understanding and respect for one another.

That was the epiphany moment for our work promoting civility, and it crystalized our mission.

## A Note on *Civility* from Stephen Henderson

I have a lot of friends who bristle when I tell them about the Great Lakes Civility Project. It's not the idea or the work. As soon as I explain what we're doing and what it's about, I can convince just about anyone of the value. Most people seem tired of the rank incivility in our politics and culture and hungry for something more palatable.

No, the problem is the word: *civility*.

For many people, it's a weapon used by the powerful to silence those they wield power over. It is a way to quell, with a single word, ordinary and acceptable protest, and it is most often used against the vulnerable in American society.

Suffragists, protesting peacefully in the early 20th century to procure the vote for women, were greeted by calls for "civility" and told they were fracturing the moral codes of productive discourse. In the 1950s and 1960s, segregationists described nearly any attempt to challenge Jim Crow as "uncivil"—everything from lunch-counter sit-ins to marches and economic boycotts.

In the mouths of the powerful, the word *civility* has too often been equated with "Sit down and shut up. Go along. Don't question."

These sentiments and directives, of course, inspire the very opposite of the goals of the Civility Project: disrespect rather than respect; muzzling rather than dialogue; the exercise of inequality rather than an acknowledgment and understanding of inherent equality.

The word *civility* needs repair in American culture, no doubt. If not for my skeptical friends, then for the greater causes of language fidelity and moral imperative.

But for our purposes in the Civility Project, the debate about the word is something of a distraction. Civility, as we define it and counsel its pursuit, is not so much about societal dynamics as individual ones.

Our pillars. The practices we have developed over 17 years. The boundaries we recognize in dialogue and arguments between us. They are about how we deal with the people in our lives, in our spaces, every day. They are about how we talk with our families, our friends and neighbors, the people in our educational or religious communities.

Our emphasis, in this project, is on people acting where they have agency and, presumably, where the power imbalance is either not outsized or not dispositive in the interaction.

The civility we are talking about is granular, not global. And it is within the grasp of even those who might bristle, as my friends do, at the wider cultural use of the term and its complicated history.

What we hope to do in the pages that follow is show people how and why more civil discussion and exchange of ideas is an earnest and achievable goal for our republic.

## Why We Do This

Incivility is killing America. And threatening our democracy.

On January 6, 2021, as Congress prepared to certify the results of the 2020 presidential election, a mob of protesters, acting on behalf of a president who wouldn't accept defeat, attacked the Capitol in Washington, DC, as lawmakers cowered in their offices.

During the 2024 presidential election, a 20-year-old, burning with the overheated passions of our politics, got a gun, climbed to a rooftop during a rally for then presidential candidate and now President Donald Trump, and fired several shots. He killed a fireman in the crowd and wounded the former president. It was the first time in nearly 40 years that such intense violence had surfaced.

These are the extreme examples, but they grow out of the everyday acts and expressions that have made the language of hate the dominant force in our culture.

We are an angry and bitter people, fractured along political, racial, and class lines, unable to talk to each other and increasingly unwilling to see value in those who believe, vote, or look differently than we do. That's the essence of incivility.

But what does civility look like?

Civility is not everyone agreeing or backing away from their beliefs in the name of cordiality or politeness. There is certainly plenty of cause to be angry about what's happening today, no matter which side of the political aisle you stand on. That anger can play a useful role in righting the many wrongs.

When we talk about civility, we are referring to the ability to engage, respectfully, despite our differences, without destroying personal relationships or destabilizing our country. In the spaces closest to us—individual interactions with friends and family, neighbors, coworkers, the people we see all the time—civility is how we manage our anger and prevent it from overwhelming the more important bonds that define our lives.

And that is the purpose of this book. Our intent is to offer a guide to maintaining civil, productive relationships across profound political divides based on our own experiences over the last nearly 20 years. We also want to help as many people as possible gain the skills needed to engage in meaningful civil conversations with the people they care about and help, relationship by relationship, return our communities to a more civil place.

As two people who are deeply committed to our personal viewpoints and whose work is rooted in our political identities, we have nonetheless found a way to disagree publicly and vigorously while also not breaking apart. As we will discuss later in the book, our goal is not for people to agree to disagree. That's avoidance.

We want them to be able to disagree while still finding value in discussing their disagreements. What we offer is a blueprint for finding the respect and understanding necessary to nurture and sustain a friendship we both consider indispensable.

## The Beginning of an Unlikely Friendship

Everyone, it seems, loves to watch a good fight.

That was the motivation for pairing us on television and radio shows and public stages after Stephen returned to Detroit in 2007 to become the editorial page editor at the *Detroit Free Press*. Nolan had been in the same job at *The Detroit News* for several years by then.

The potential for our joint appearances to produce fireworks was irresistible to producers. A conservative and a liberal. A Democrat and a Republican. An African American and a White guy. Put us together and we were bound to scrap, right? And we did—with the intensity everyone anticipated.

The first time we met was on the set of Devin Scillian's *Flashpoint* show on WDIV-TV. We showed up thinking we already knew everything we needed to know about each other based on what we had read or heard.

"I thought Steve would be an insufferable, knee-jerk liberal," Nolan says. "He certainly was passionate about his progressive positions. But he wasn't at all what I expected. He wasn't defensive. He was very open to considering other views, and sometimes in surprising ways. I appreciated that. And I almost immediately sensed this was someone I'd like to get to know better."

Stephen had a similar reaction: "I didn't know Nolan at all. Pretty quickly, I noticed that he was not typical in the way he approached things. I wasn't really surprised by his conservative opinions, but I was surprised by the way he got there and his open-mindedness to the possibility there could be other ways to come at it. He didn't think giving real consideration to what someone else has to say weakens your own position."

Pragmatism was something we shared from the beginning—the belief that holding strong principles is a fine thing, but ultimately, they shouldn't be allowed to become an obstacle to reaching a consensus on a solution.

Also, we are both willing to call out our own side when we feel it's necessary. We don't march in lockstep with either the conservative or progressive establishment. That opens the door for more productive discussions.

At the time of our introduction, Nolan had a public affairs show on Detroit Public Television. His cohost often had scheduling conflicts, so he started asking Stephen to fill in when she couldn't make a taping.

"It was just the two of us talking about issues," Stephen says. "I think we both recognized at that point that the way we were able to talk about these things was really different."

There was definite on-air chemistry. What set our interactions apart from similar programs is that while we got loud and sometimes angry, we weren't trying to destroy one another. We weren't all about scoring points at the other's expense, nor did we aim to embarrass each other.

We developed a comfort level, a trust, that allowed us to go after one another without fear that a line would be crossed that we couldn't come back from. Rather than something we dreaded, the debates became a thing we really enjoyed.

Early on, we realized we wanted the same outcomes: good government; a fairer, more prosperous society; a better future for our children; and a nation that stands on the high ground. Knowing we want to get to the same place in the end and that our friction lies mostly in how to get there takes some of the tension out of our interactions.

It helps to get to know one another outside of politics. As we said, we both appreciate good bourbon. It's really difficult to harbor hard feelings toward someone with whom you're sharing a glass of fine Kentucky whiskey.

And we both recognize that regardless of political perspective, in a job like the ones we hold, people are continuously coming after you. There's always going to be a large segment of your audience or readership that simply hates you for what you say or write.

That can be wearying, particularly on days when the attacks are relentless. When *The Detroit News* refused to endorse either Donald Trump or Hillary Clinton in the 2016 presidential race, choosing a third-party candidate instead, the fire came from both the right and left. The newspaper's traditional conservative readers felt betrayed, and progressives were certain our third-party choice would assure Trump a Michigan win.

Similarly, when the *Detroit Free Press* gave its support to former Gov. Rick Snyder, a Republican, over Democratic nominees Virg Bernero in 2010 and Mark Shauer in 2014, Stephen endured a firestorm from his progressive audience.

"It can be a very difficult thing to go through day after day," Stephen says. "There is some empathy there, as well as some understanding, of what it takes to do this job."

For our work, we've had to develop strong opinions and defend them with confidence. There's really no room for wishy-washy viewpoints, particularly in a competitive market. But some self-doubt is healthy. Our friendship has benefited from our ability to use each other as sounding boards.

"I always start the opinion-forming process with the assumption that I may be wrong," Nolan says. "And so I'm looking for information that affirms or refutes my position. I want to consider other ideas and counterviews to have something to weigh my opinions against. Steve often serves that purpose."

"Columnists often live in an echo chamber," says Stephen. "We don't. That was one of the ways we found commonality and became friends."

There likely would be some value in attacking each other publicly and personally. Our individual audiences would love for us to affirm their beliefs that the other is an ogre. We don't do that and never have. Rather, we have each other's backs. We speak up for one another, publicly and privately; advocate for one another; and most importantly, trust each other.

"When people talk to me about Nolan, it's the thing they always ask about," says Stephen. "'How did you end up being so close with that guy?' Because it is unlikely. It's just not common, either in the newspaper context or in the political context."

"The respect I have for Steve starts with my admiration for his work," says Nolan. "In my opinion, he's the best writer, the best thinker, in Michigan, in Detroit, and among the best in this business."

Stephen wrote the foreword for Nolan's book, *Little Red Hen: A Collection of Columns from Detroit's Conservative Voice*. He focused on how we impact each other's work. "I had to pay attention to what was going on in his shop because I wanted our shop to keep up," Stephen says. "You don't do that with someone you don't respect or whose work you don't respect, right? Often, you're just ignoring the competition, but that was never the case when we were in those jobs."

No two people are likely to disagree on everything all of the time. In our case, we've found a number of opportunities to work together on causes we share.

One such collaboration came a few years ago during the downtown Detroit Fireworks. Leading up to the annual celebration, the Detroit Police Department and City Council were weighing a curfew on unaccompanied teens that would have kept them away from the riverfront.

Both of us wrote about the issue and shared the perspective that it was really bad optics for the city to round up Black children, load them into vans and buses, and take them away from the festivities while White kids were flooding into the city with their families.

The columns led to a meeting with then police chief James Craig and community leaders. It ended with an agreement to set aside a supervised area, with activities sponsored by local businesses, where teens could gather to safely watch the fireworks. No kids were arrested during that year's event, and no incidents were reported.

We teamed up again, both in our columns and on our television program, to call attention to the fact that African Americans were largely being marginalized in Detroit's amazing comeback.

We took that issue on together after a local business group stopped by our TV set with a group of 50 young people it identified as "Detroit's future leaders." Only one was Black. That just didn't seem right to us. We believe our voices on the issue were more impactful because we were speaking from different sides of the philosophical divide while delivering the same message.

While we never viewed our friendship as a curiosity, other people did. We fielded lots of questions challenging the sincerity of our relationship. Though we had many mutual friends, we also had a lot of friends who wouldn't think about talking with each other.

So we decided to bring them together in a sort of experiment. We booked the back room of a downtown bar and each invited 10 friends who shared our respective political orientations. Guests would toss $20 in a hat to cover the tab. We did this every month, usually inviting a guest speaker to give a brief talk on politics or policy and take questions.

What began with a handful of people quickly grew into standing-room-only sessions. These Bourbon Nights were the precursor to the Great Lakes Civility Project. They eventually became a staple of the annual Mackinac Policy Conference hosted by the Detroit Regional Chamber. The Off the Record, On the Island parties draw hundreds of conference attendees.

The response still surprises us. "I hear all the time about people who are apprehensive about talking to somebody they disagree with because they think it'll end up in a fight," says Stephen.

"I don't think I realized the formal nature of those concerns and the willingness that people have to actually talk about ways to do it differently. I figured we'd get people who were interested. I didn't think for a second we'd get the number of people involved that we've had or that it would go on as long as it has."

Not once in all the years we've been hosting Bourbon Nights have there been angry encounters between guests. Civility has prevailed—surprising, considering that alcohol is a key ingredient of these gatherings. We encourage people not to bunker down at Bourbon Night. The price of entry is a willingness to talk to someone you might be tempted to avoid in another setting. Most people welcome the opportunity. But they don't often take the chance. A Pew Research Center survey found that two-thirds of Democrats and just over half of Republicans say they have few friends, if any, across the political aisle.

Based on what we've seen and heard during Bourbon Nights and in our Civility Sessions, there's a far-reaching desire to do better, yet an uncertainty about how to start. Avoidance is the path of least resistance. It's also the least productive choice. People recognize there's a lot of hostility in our society, and it bothers them. They also feel powerless to do much about it. And in their own lives, they want to heal relationships that have been broken by political differences.

We have figured out how to stay friends and have lots of places where we can interact that don't have anything to do with politics, but we can also still argue about politics and policy—argue strenuously, passionately—and never get to the point where we can't talk to each other anymore.

Most importantly, we've learned friends don't have to be ideological carbon copies. There's more to us than just our politics.

There's bourbon, for one. For us, it's always a good conversation starter.

## The Civility Project

The idea for the Civility Project grew out of a session we did a few years ago for National Public Radio's StoryCorps project.

We sat down in a mobile recording studio, just the two of us, and talked for an hour about our upbringings, the people who influenced us, the significant events that helped shape the way we process facts on our way to forming opinions.

We each started life in very modest households that teetered on the edge of poverty. Our common path upward was education, hard work, and a healthy fear of the wolf at the door. Both of our families came to Detroit from the rural South, lured by automotive jobs.

Stephen's family became deeply involved in the union and civil rights movements, rising through the ranks of the United Auto Workers union and eventually Detroit's political structure. That informs his belief that the institutions of society, when challenged and held accountable, are the best hope for creating fair and equitable communities.

Nolan's roots are set in Kentucky's Appalachian foothills, populated by fiercely independent people whose distrust of government was a cultural touchstone and who earned everything they had with muscle and sweat. That shaped his belief in self-reliance and the virtue of free markets.

The more we learned about each other, the better we understood what made one of us a conservative and the other a progressive. We also came to the important realization that two people can look at the same set of facts, apply their individual experiences and values, and come up with different opinions. That doesn't make either one evil or ignorant.

Though we may advocate for different solutions, the outcomes we want for our community are mostly the same. We have learned to have intense discussions without trying to convert each other. We gave up a long time ago on any hope of bringing the other to an epiphany. We're always going to disagree. And that's OK.

The Great Lakes Civility Project began in 2019, as the political tenor in the United States reached a feverish pitch. We had been speaking informally about our friendship for a couple of years. With the nation seemingly on the verge of ripping at the seams, we decided to step up our efforts. With the help of author and marketing expert Lynne Golodner, we established the Great Lakes Civility Project and began offering virtual and in-person programs.

The timing was both awkward and fortunate. Just as we were about to launch our very first program, the COVID-19 pandemic made it impossible to meet in person. But the rapid adoption of virtual meeting technology allowed us to reach more groups in more places. We have spoken to audiences as large as 500 people over Zoom, in states from coast to coast, north to south.

Our mission is to impress upon other Americans that while we may disagree on many issues, we agree on the importance of our relationship. This is something that anyone can extrapolate and take into their own relationships and communities.

"It never occurred to us that we couldn't be friends because we disagree," says Nolan. "We've never avoided conversation, we never pulled punches, we enjoy the mix-up."

## Chapter Insights

- 66 percent of Democrats and 50 percent of Republicans say they have few friends, if any, across the political aisle.
- Focus on similar outcomes and debate *how* you got there.
- Civility is the ability to engage, respectfully, despite our differences, without destroying personal relationships or destabilizing our country.

## Recommended Actions

- Read these pages with an open mind. Be prepared to consider new ways of thinking about and looking at conversations.
- Get ready to examine how you came to your beliefs and political stances—and be open to learning about how others arrived there as well!

---

### "WHO YOU ARE" WORKSHEET

Use this worksheet to delve into your identity, background, and influences! This will serve as a foundation for understanding your own perspective and political stance as you learn more about interacting with people who may believe differently.

What is your first memory of politics?

What was your early exposure to political views?

Who were the most influential voices in your family or neighborhood regarding politics?

Today, what is most important to your political opinion?

Are there specific issues that inform your voting decisions? If so, how did you decide on your current stance on these issues? What factors, influences, or information led you to your current views?

What is most frustrating to you about politics today?

Why might you strive to achieve civility when it comes to politics?

> Is there a person in your life with whom you could begin to have conversations toward building civility and understanding? Would they be open to this?
>
> How might you be a voice of change in your community and bring civility into the political sphere? What can you do to diminish the divided rhetoric?

# 1

# What Civility Is and Why It Matters

When we talk about civility, we don't necessarily mean being nice or avoiding confrontation. Vigorous debate can get loud, even angry. We define civility not as politeness and certainly not as remaining calm and silent in the face of injustice. And we certainly don't mean agreeing to disagree. That suggests avoidance, and that's not what we want at all.

Our definition of civility is having conversations about things you disagree on without letting hate enter into the equation. Civility is the ability to engage without animosity, without personal attacks, and without degrading those with whom you disagree.

It's "disagreeing without disrespect, seeking common ground as a starting point for dialogue about differences, listening past one's preconceptions, and teaching others to do the same," says Larry Hanson, CEO and executive director of the Georgia Municipal Association.[1] "Civility is the hard work of staying present even with those with whom we have deep-rooted and fierce disagreement."

That's not to say good manners and a standard of etiquette don't matter. They're always helpful. But not essential.

---

[1] www.gacities.com/Initiatives/Civility.aspx#:~:text=What%20is%20Civility%3F,others%20to%20do%20the%20same.

Those who have watched us debate issues might consider our tone anything but civil. We're often fiery. And while that may make some onlookers uncomfortable, we're just fine with it because we have established lines we won't cross. They may not be visible to onlookers, but we see them clearly.

In a general sense, those lines exist to keep us from treating others in discriminatory or hateful ways. And to not bully or degrade. Respect depends on seeing each other as equals. If you don't believe that another person has the same rights as you do, how can you ever engage in a meaningful discussion with them?

That's why we always encourage people to begin by getting to know the person behind the politics. Only then can you engage in an honest exploration of different viewpoints from a place of curiosity and a desire for understanding.

It may be a tougher ask today than ever before because as Americans, we are angrier than we've been in a long while. But history offers reassurance as well as warnings. In the 1790s, citizens of the new nation were accusing one another of losing their "true American principles." Sound familiar?

Protesters torched buildings and challenged the validity of their leaders, including America's first president, George Washington. "If ever a nation was debauched by a man, the American nation has been debauched by Washington.... If ever a nation has suffered from the improper influence of a man, the American nation has suffered from the influence of Washington," wrote the *Philadelphia Aurora General Advertiser* in a December 1796 article.[2]

Anger used to be something to be embarrassed about, writes James Averil, a psychology professor at the University of Massachusetts at Amherst in the *Atlantic*. Most people were ashamed to exhibit public anger, believing it to be to the detriment of society. Anger, he said, "is one of the densest forms of communication. It

---

[2] washingtonpapers.org/fake-news-newspapers-and-george-washingtons-second-presidential-administration/.

conveys more information, more quickly, than almost any other emotion."

That's an effective way to get people to listen, to speak honestly, and to accommodate the complaints of others. Anger empowers people to do difficult things and builds creativity, leading people to find solutions they might not have noticed when they were calmer.

It's safe to say that anger is an essential American value, a defining part of our national identity. Anger fueled the overthrow of the British monarchy. Our frontier was pockmarked by gun battles to resolve disputes. Even our Bill of Rights "guarantees that we can argue with one another in the public square, through a free press and in open court."

But, writes the author Charles Duhigg, winner of a 2013 Pulitzer Prize while at the *New York Times*, this essential American anger is different than what we are currently witnessing in that today, it is aimed at groups of people we don't know and about whom we can fabricate whole mythologies that fuel increasing levels of fierce emotion.

"Anger seems to have consumed American politics," Duhigg writes. As recently as 2012, less than half of voters were angry at the other party's presidential nominee. By 2016, nearly 70 percent were.

Unresolved anger can evolve into moral indignation. And if the angry fellow doesn't believe he's being heard or taken seriously, that indignation can morph into a desire for revenge against perceived enemies.

Those managing the political machines are using our individual and collective rage for their own purposes—to get their candidates elected—without regard for the lasting damage it is doing to the American public.

While most Americans say they do not condone violence, more Americans are embracing strong partisanship, which can lead to a debilitating and dangerous anger. The antidote is encouraging more personal contact between those who disagree. If people who profess to hate one another can have a conversation in a respectful, controlled manner, they have a chance of achieving civility. They may never agree, but they may come to see the humanity in one another, and their extreme anger will mellow into something less threatening.

In his 1964 essay "The Paranoid Style in American Politics," Richard Hofstadter said that "American politics has often been an arena for angry minds."[3] Many Americans like to think that things used to be better, more civil, more aligned. Maybe that isn't true. Maybe part of the American way is to struggle with discord, to meet it head-on, and to grapple with notions of truth and justice. Today's divisions are certainly different from those of earlier eras. But it's part of our DNA to feud. Our challenge is to not let it become our unraveling.

## Why Civility Matters

Practicing civility isn't just an exercise in being nice. It's essential to our survival as a free and democratic society.

The foundation of the Great Lakes Civility Project is a deep desire to improve understanding between people and tamp down the suspicions and fear that too often lead to hate. We are promoting civility because we believe there is no greater threat to America than hatred.

Civility is part of the human compact we have with one another for managing disagreements. There will always be differences of opinion. But you don't get to club your neighbors over the head because they don't think the way you do. Building a culture of civility will help us maintain a healthy society despite our political, cultural, economic, and religious differences.

And yet, civility itself is not the end goal. Forced politeness without productive interaction will accomplish little. The ultimate

---

[3] harpers.org/archive/1964/11/the-paranoid-style-in-american-politics/.

objective is a functioning republic in which we can coexist while meeting our shared challenges. Today, our politics and our government are increasingly dysfunctional because we have adopted a no-compromise, winner-take-all mindset that is not conducive to problem-solving.

That, and we have stopped talking to each other. "What we have here is a failure to communicate," to quote a line from the 1967 film *Cool Hand Luke*.

We can't hold together as a people if we are unable or unwilling to work together. That doesn't mean abandoning individual principles or sacrificing core beliefs. It does require committing to consensus building and recognizing, as former president Ronald Reagan said, "If you got 75 or 80 percent of what you were asking for, I say you take it and fight for the rest later."

Sacrificing ideological purity for pragmatism is the only path toward progress. In a nation with such a diversity of views, it is irrational and irresponsible to expect your view to prevail 100 percent of the time. We have to learn to reengage in the give-and-take of republican governing and commit to living with the results.

One of the best examples of the dangers of an all-or-nothing approach was our response to the COVID-19 pandemic. The nation faced an existential threat, one without a precedent we could follow.

We had no idea what would work and what wouldn't. Instead of pulling together to find answers, we broke into partisan camps and attacked one another. We refused to use the trial-and-error process to learn from our mistakes and instead locked ourselves into solutions based on which political leaders originated them rather than the results they produced. Whether it was masks, medicines, or vaccines, we dug in and wouldn't budge.

We bickered while our friends and family members were dying. And worse, on both the left and right, we sought opportunities for political gain and grandstanding.

The reality that we could not work together to defeat a plague that was wreaking mass devastation should cause us great concern.

We undoubtedly will face another such threat, and we are no better positioned to meet it with a united front.

This is what happens when incivility reigns, when we refuse to listen to someone simply because they are speaking from the other side of the divide, when half the country believes it can force its will on the other because it holds the reins of power.

Partisanship is a poor weapon against pandemics. Or terrorism. Or environmental catastrophes. Or any of the other forces, current and future, that place human survival at risk.

When you can't put the country first, you put democracy in jeopardy. Still, we have hope for the future of America because we have faith in the American people.

In the scores of Civility Sessions we've done since 2020, with groups ranging from atheists to zookeepers and representing every possible philosophy and partisan stance, what they all have in common is the desire to do better. There is a recognition of the harm incivility is doing to our country and the hurt it is inflicting on our personal relationships. People are unified in their desire to get to a brighter place.

We are also heartened that ours is just one of many, many civility efforts underway nationwide. Americans are starting to organize efforts to push back against the poisonous partisanship that has as its goal keeping us fearful and divided. They understand the need to be proactive in preserving our democracy.

Fortunately, individuals are not powerless. In fact, they hold the answer. Returning civility to our society starts with one-on-one engagement, practicing civility in personal relationships and in the spaces where we have agency.

This is not a quick process. But the more you treat people with civility, the more likely they are to respond in a like manner. Don't discount the very real multiplier effect. It's not just you out there trying to bring civility to your whole community. It starts with you and builds into a group committed to behaving civilly.

This country is designed for grassroots change because the individual is empowered by our Constitution. Small groups and individuals can begin big movements—we've seen that over and over again throughout our history. Starting small; taking it one conversation, one relationship, one community at a time; and persisting with dedication to a purpose and a cause has always been the way we introduce and solidify significant ideas.

What does that look like? First, stop giving your vote to politicians who preach hate, who default to fearmongering instead of offering a vision for healing our nation and the communities within it. There are plenty of those on both sides of the aisle. Send them packing. At the ballot box, reward hope and reject hate.

In 2026, we will celebrate 250 years since the start of the American Revolution. That will make the United States the oldest surviving democracy on the planet. We have an obligation to future Americans to pass along that democracy intact and thriving.

Personally, the two of us stand on different points of the political spectrum and have vastly different ideas for how to make that happen. But we love this country with equal passion and share a commitment to its prosperity. We recognize there is a good deal of disappointment in where we are as a nation. But in our experience, most people still want to be proud Americans and part of this experiment in how a diverse nation can live and govern in a way that benefits everyone.

Like us, they don't necessarily have the same ideas about what that means or how to get there, but most people would never say, "I'm ready for something else." Rather, they are saying, "I want this to work for me." The challenge is moving them to the point where they want it to work for all their neighbors too.

One of the greatest assaults on our nation's endurance happened on January 6, 2021. But it didn't work. A key revelation from that dark day is the number of people on both sides of the political aisle who acted to make sure the United States of America, as a democracy, did not crumble.

Civility is the fuel that powers a robust democracy. That's why we started the Great Lakes Civility Project. We hope it will contribute in some small way to moving America beyond this perilous period in which we are living.

## Chapter Insights

- Our definition of civility is having conversations about things you disagree on without letting hate enter into the equation.
- Anger is an essential American value—a defining part of our national identity.
- Respect depends on seeing each other as equals.
- Get to know the person behind the politics.

## Recommended Actions

- Returning civility to our society begins with one-on-one engagement.
- Practice civility in personal relationships and in the spaces where we have agency.
- Think about the people in your life who might be open to such a conversation.

---

### QUESTIONS FOR YOU

These questions might help articulate the emotions behind your perspectives, which is so important, as reactions are often driven by emotions rather than curiosity or rational thought. The answers to these questions can be a starting point for strengthening interaction with people you care about and bringing you closer to civility on tough topics. Are there any surprises?

> What makes you angry about politics or the state of American life today?
>
> Do you believe that things used to be better in America? If so, how do you imagine they were better in the past than today?
>
> How do you respond to other people expressing their anger?
>
> Are you willing to engage in civil discourse with people who hold different opinions or beliefs than you? If yes, why does that excite you? If no, what scares you about it?
>
> What would you hope to gain from engaging in civil conversation with people who hold different views?

# 2

# The Causes and Effects of Incivility

Incivility leads to hate. Hate leads to dehumanization. And dehumanization leads to history's worst atrocities.

It's a proven timeline that begins with an ember and eventually engulfs society in flames. Keeping the spark from becoming an inferno requires making sure it doesn't find the fuel it needs to spread. That fuel is fear and hatred.

The progression is illustrated on posters of pyramids that hang on the walls of the Zekelman Holocaust Center in Farmington Hills, Michigan. One pyramid illustrates the course of society toward genocide; the other, the pathway to peace.

The bottom layer of the pyramid to peace is civility, and at the bottom of the pyramid to genocide, it's incivility.

"There are two halves to the pyramid to peace," says Rabbi Eli Mayerfeld, the center's director. "The individual and the collective: What can I do, and what can *we* do? Both sides are necessary. If you want to build a country with a peaceful society, you need individuals acting with civility."

That begins, the rabbi says, with caring about others, valuing life, and committing to engagement. The building blocks include the things we talk about in the Great Lakes Civility Project: creating understanding through respectful dialogue, dropping negative assumptions, and recognizing that opinions are the product of an individual's experiences.

"These are normal human behaviors," Mayerfeld says. "That's what we need from individuals to build a peaceful society."

Mayerfeld emphasizes the importance of committing acts of altruism to demonstrate a focus on others rather than solely on our own interests.

"Our individual choices make a difference," he says. "The activity of individual civility grows into a community collective."

The community side of the pyramid requires inclusive policies that protect the rights of minorities and a government that recognizes the equality of all its citizens. In addition, we must move away from the winner-take-all approach to governing.

"People think that if we get to 51 percent, we get our way. That's not how democracies work," Mayerfeld says.

Rather, a thriving democratic government stresses consensus building and compromise that takes into account the needs and concerns of the minority party. Neither side gets everything it wants, but everyone gets something. The greater the level of cooperation, the better the chance of progress that benefits the whole.

## Partisanship

The story of the relationship between Ronald Reagan and Tip O'Neill, who was the powerful Speaker of the House during the former president's tenure, is part of America's political legend.

It is often cited to emphasize the lost civility in American politics. The Republican president and the Democratic Speaker were ideologically as different as night and day.

O'Neill was a New Deal liberal, Reagan the torchbearer of the modern conservative movement. During the 1980s, they often found themselves locked in a continuous struggle over the direction of the country.

Compromise didn't come easy. But it did come because each man placed the good of the country ahead of their partisan interests.

They were able to reach a consensus because they shared a profound mutual respect and a familiarity that allowed them to work through their differences. Their friendship was important to them, and they aimed to maintain it despite the intensity of their political battles.

According to an oft-repeated anecdote, Reagan answered phone calls from O'Neill by asking, "Tip, is it after 6 p.m.?" Working hours were for knocking each other in the head on the political battlefield. After hours were for sharing a drink and a laugh.

Former talk show host Chris Matthews, who was O'Neill's chief of staff, writes about their relationship in his book *Tip and the Gipper: When Politics Worked*. "There were rules in those days," Matthews says. "Tip would say, 'I'll cut a deal on Social Security if you let me focus on taxing the wealthier people.'"

The trust they built through nurturing their friendship made them more effective public servants. They understood and had a profound appreciation for the fact that the American people didn't put them in their powerful positions for them to wage destructive ideological battles. They wanted them to produce results on their behalf. Perhaps no two political opposites in the modern era ever worked so well together to advance America's interests.

That dedication to serving people over party is what's missing in today's politics. The opposite motivation has taken root: nothing is more important to those sitting in the country's political chambers than gaining and maintaining partisan power. Partisanship has poisoned our politics and rendered our political system nearly useless in meeting the challenges facing our nation.

The presidential choices presented to voters in the past two election cycles are evidence of the failure of our political system.

Nearly three-quarters of Americans said they wanted someone other than Donald Trump and Joe Biden on the ballot.

But two political parties unresponsive to the desires of the people gave them Trump and Biden's vice president, Kamala Harris, anyway. Neither candidate had a chance of uniting the people because the partisan interests that kept them in power would not allow them to do the things necessary to bring the country together.

Chief among them is governing from the middle and committing to bipartisan consensus. That requires relationships like the one shared by O'Neill and Reagan, built on trust and respect.

They still exist in Washington—witness the close and cooperative bond between Debbie Dingell and Fred Upton, who wrote the foreword to this book. But they are scarce.

Congress's Problem Solvers Caucus, created as a tool for fostering consensus governing and ending the winner-take-all mindset in Washington, has just 31 Republicans and 32 Democratic members in the House, out of 435 representatives. These few members are all that are left of the moderates in Congress.

Attempts at true bipartisanship are often punished. Democrats and Republicans have subjected members who don't line up 100 percent with their party to primary challenges to demonstrate the risks of showing anything but absolute loyalty. GOP Reps. Liz Cheney and Peter Meijer were driven out of their House seats for opposing former president Donald Trump. Texas Rep. Henry Cuellar, the only self-identified pro-life Democrat in the House, faced a primary challenge from his own party in 2022 because he sided with Republicans on antiabortion measures. Democratic Senators Joe Manchin from West Virginia and Kyrstin Sinema from Arizona, both representing conservative states, were regularly attacked for voting with Republicans, and both ultimately left the Democratic Party to become independents.

The two of us have interviewed hundreds of candidates for office during our careers. Nearly every would-be politician who makes the case for our endorsement pledges that if elected, they will work on behalf of their constituents and not their party.

Very few remember that promise when they get to Washington, DC, or Lansing. Once they're seated, the pressure to swear allegiance to the party's interests is too great.

Partisan leaders hold enormous power over the success of their members. Going along assures a nicer office and more influential and lucrative committee assignments. In contrast, drifting too far from the party's expectations risks landing in an office in the basement next to the boiler and a spot on a committee that has zero appeal to potential donors.

There's danger even in demonstrating civility toward a member of the other party. Former New Jersey governor Chris Christie, a Republican, was roundly derided by his party for greeting Democratic president Barack Obama with a hug and a thank-you when he arrived in his state in 2012 to view the damage caused by Hurricane Sandy. It was a basic act of civility, of humanity, and yet it still dogged Christie more than a decade later when he was making a presidential run.

More recently, Republican House Speaker Kevin McCarthy was ousted by the extremists in the GOP caucus for reaching across the aisle to forge a bipartisan spending deal to keep the government from shutting down. Democrats refused to come to his rescue, even though it meant scuttling the deal they urged McCarthy to make.

A few years ago, we were approached about doing a Civility Session with incoming members of the new Michigan legislature. Term limits were still in place then, and lawmakers came and went so fast they didn't have a chance to get to know—and trust—each other.

The idea was that if legislators from different parties could sit across from each other and talk about who they are and what motivates them, they could build the respect and familiarity necessary for consensus governing.

The project never got off the ground. When we approached the leader of one of the chambers, he told us, "I'm not sure I want my members talking with the other side. It might make it harder for me to control them." It was about as honest a comment as we've heard from a politician—and a perfect explanation of how incivility serves partisan political ambitions.

While American politics have always been confrontational, we have reached a level rarely seen even in the most divisive periods of our history. Several factors contribute to the current hostility, but none more so than partisanship.

Politicians today are not so much identified with their ideological philosophy—progressive, moderate, conservative—as they are with their political party. They are Republicans or Democrats first, and any individual principles they hold must be shaped to fit the party's dogma. Diversity of views isn't tolerated, and dissenters are driven out. How many pro-life Democrats do you know? How many pro-choice Republicans? If they harbor those views, they can't say so publicly out of fear they'll lose their standing in their parties—and their seats.

It wasn't always like that. Getting a bill passed through Congress or the legislature once required building coalitions across party lines between like-minded Republicans and Democrats. Now, such cross-party vote whipping is rare. The degrees of difference on the ideological scale are small between members of the same party. Rockefeller Republicans have all but disappeared, and there are fewer than 10 Blue Dog Democrats left in Congress.

Partisan redistricting practices have left moderate and independent voters with a far smaller voice in the governing process. When the two parties collude to draw congressional and legislative districts that pack their supporters together, candidates don't have to compete for the middle.

This so-called gerrymandering gives rise to extremism and policymaking solely designed to satisfy the desire of the politician's base. There is little incentive for consensus building.

Nowhere is money more the root of all evil than in politics.[1] Since the Supreme Court's 2010 *Citizens United* ruling that outside groups can spend unlimited amounts on elections, politics has become a big-money enterprise. As rivers of cash have poured into the political process, it has shifted the balance of power toward large corporations, unions, and other special interest groups and away from individual voters.

A 2023 Pew Research survey found that just 9 percent of Americans believe the people in their districts have the most influence on members of Congress, while 80 percent believe their representatives are most responsive to their large financial backers.

US House and Senate candidates reported raising $2.4 billion in the 2022 election cycle; political parties collected $1.4 billion, and political action committees (PACs), the least accountable source of funding, added $5.5 billion, according to the Federal Election Commission. In the 2018 midterm election, the average winning US Senate candidate spent $15 million from all sources, and the average victorious House candidate spent $2 million. Vice President Kamala Harris and her backers spent more than $1 billion on her unsuccessful run for the presidency in 2024.

Fundraising is the central preoccupation of members of Congress. The amount of money involved creates a win-at-all-costs environment and distances politicians from accountability to their voters. PACs, which aren't supposed to coordinate their efforts with those of the candidates they support, can create the vilest attack ads while the politicians deny responsibility.

That's led to the proliferation of political advertising that is nearly completely detached from the truth and, often, the bounds of decency. It has coarsened our political discourse and deepened our divide. Sadly, the attack ads continue because they work. Research

---

[1] This quote paraphrases a biblical reference: "For the love of money is the root of all evil: which while some coveted after, they have erred from the faith, and pierced themselves through with many sorrows" (1 Timothy 6:10 KJV).

has found the anger evoked by attack ads is more influential than any other emotion that motivates voters.[2]

The late political shock jock Rush Limbaugh became among the most influential figures in America by destroying all the rules of civility. The immense popularity of his radio show was fueled by demeaning and demonizing those who held views that were different from his and those of his fan base.

The intellectual debate of ideas was shouted down and replaced by name-calling and insults that have become the vocabulary of today's politics. The notion that the other side might have something of value to offer was not tolerated.

The show became an echo chamber of hate that spawned a host of copycats on both the right and left and has steadily moved from radio to cable television to the internet. Now, the places where we can find respectful dialogue and the thoughtful give-and-take necessary for reaching an informed opinion are few. Far more common are forums that foster conspiracy theories and plant seeds of hate, where fearmongering and lies flourish.

The Bill of Rights Institute recently published an article from Alisha Sanders, an eighth grade teacher from Gettysburg, Pennsylvania, who advocated for strong civics education as an antidote for civility. "I say this sincerely and with urgency: teaching civics today is one of the most important things we can do to save humanity and restore civility," she writes.

Today's students, she says, "are more aware of current events and seek to understand the historical causes of them. They want to dive deeper. They thrive on interacting with each other and get excited when they learn and begin to understand their civil liberties and civil rights and how genuine argumentation doesn't have to cause pain."[3]

We concur with her assessment. Knowledge and understanding are the best weapons against fear and ignorance.

2 www.ncbi.nlm.nih.gov/pmc/articles/PMC8793837/.
3 www.ncbi.nlm.nih.gov/pmc/articles/PMC8793837/.

Robust civics classes that encourage discussion and debate about current events are proven to increase the likelihood that students will continue to engage in political discussion as adults and will be more likely to participate in the democratic process.[4]

Unfortunately, civics classes are de-emphasized in public education in favor of STEM courses and other priorities. It's as if we expect our children to know instinctively what it means to be an American and that there are rules that must be followed and rights that must be observed, chief among them free speech.

Yet teaching the nation's fundamental ideals and the rights and expectations of its citizens remains a low priority. The *Hill* reports that only 7 states require a full year of civics instruction in high school, and 13 have no requirement at all. The federal government spends $50 a student for STEM education and only $0.05 per student on civics.

As a result of decades of neglect, nearly one-third of Americans can't name the three branches of government, according to the Annenberg Constitution Day Civics Survey. When such a large percentage of the citizenry lacks the basic knowledge of how their government works, as well as of their rights and responsibilities as citizens, it makes them easier to manipulate by those who stand to benefit from setting Americans against one another.

Scholars Pete Peterson and Jack Miller see a direct link between the rise of hateful ideologies and the decline in "teaching our nation's founding principles and history in a non-ideological way. American civics and history, rightly taught, is a powerful tool for fighting all 'isms.'"[5] Without such training, the understanding of what makes us unique as Americans diminishes, and ideas that run counter to those foundational values are allowed to flourish—and along with them, hate and intolerance.

4 ies.ed.gov/ncee/rel/Products/Region/midwest/Ask-A-REL/10183 (URL inactive).
5 jackmillercenter.org/news/how-civics-can-counter-antisemitism-in-campus.

We have seen clearly where a twisted interpretation of patriotism combined with a skewed understanding of the Constitution leads: straight to the US Capitol on January 6, 2021, where for the first time in our history, a mob composed of our own citizens attempted to stop the peaceful transfer of the presidency.

## Rising Hate

Rabbi Mayerfeld is troubled by signs he sees in America today. Our society is moving up the wrong pyramid.

Tribalism is goading us into distinctly divided communities of interest, where members are isolated from groups that are not theirs and intolerance of others takes firm root. Cross-communication has withered. This environment breeds fear and is ripe for demonization.

The rabbi points to growing antisemitism as fair warning of what's ahead.

"Look at the news reports coming out of New York and elsewhere," he says. "Violent acts against Jews are increasing. You see videos of a Jew and a non-Jew passing on the street, and the non-Jewish person hits the Jew in the head for no reason. Jews are always the canaries in the coal mine."

Rabbi Mayerfeld's father's family left Germany in 1938 as Nazism took firm hold in that country. Memories of the family's experience with extreme antisemitism lingered into his own childhood. As a boy, when he went out in public, he was urged by his parents to wear a baseball cap instead of a yarmulke to avoid harassment.

That has a familiar ring. Today, Jewish students on campuses are removing their Star of David pendants and taking other steps to hide their Jewishness to avoid harassment and even violence. A new generation is swapping religious head coverings for ball caps.

"In 2024 in Michigan, I shouldn't have to cover my yarmulke," Mayerfeld says. "My concern is what's going on today is of a piece with what happened then."

Hatred, whether against Jews or other groups, never holds in place. It begins with simmering resentment and grows into a boiling rage. At that point, keeping it contained becomes extremely difficult.

"Once you dehumanize, you can justify anything," Mayerfeld says. "It's a very scary moment when we are starting to see those first steps in the United States."

Mayerfeld says he thinks often of the late commentator Charles Krauthammer's final column in the *Washington Post* titled "The Guardrails Hold."[6] In it, the conservative intellectual made the argument that America's institution of democracy was strong enough to meet the challenges it faced at the time of the column's writing in 2017.

The question is whether that's still true today.

"That's something I'm always looking at," Mayerfeld says. "As a society, are there things we declare as not acceptable? I look at hatred of Jews, and there are behaviors, public comments by public figures, that just should not be acceptable. We need to create a society where those kinds of things are not acceptable. It's up to individuals to say so."

While Jews have been the most persistent victims of genocide, there are many other examples of peoples being wiped away by the lust for territory, a tyrannical quest for power, and pure hatred. And the examples are hardly ancient history.

A series of ongoing genocidal movements rooted in racial hatred of Black Africans are ongoing in Sudan.[7] Between 2003 and 2005, an estimated 200,000 Fur, Zaghawa, and Masalit people were killed by the Arab African–controlled government. A second wave of killings resulting from a civil war between the government and Christians and Black animists displaced one million people between 1956 and 1967. The murderous campaigns by the government against the ethnic

---

6 www.washingtonpost.com/opinions/the-guardrails-hold/2017/08/03/fcfc157c-7877-11e7-9eac-d56bd5568db8_story.html.
7 worldwithoutgenocide.org/genocides-and-conflicts/darfur-genocide.

minorities also feature rape and starvation, leading to the conflict in Sudan being labeled the worst humanitarian crisis in the world today.

Also in Africa, the ethnic Hutu people of Rwanda in 1994 set about to cleanse their nation of its Tutsi population.[8] The Hutus whipped their followers into a lethal frenzy with hate messages broadcast on state radio. Armed Tutsi rebels from neighboring countries moved into Rwanda and ended the murderous rampage, but not before 800,000 people—one-tenth of the nation's population—had been killed.

Ethnic hatred also drove the genocide in Bosnia and Herzegovina in the 1990s.[9] Serbs intent on eliminating the country's Muslim population and emboldened by the election of one of their own, Slobodan Milošević, as president, moved against the Muslim residents of Bosnia, who had declared their independence. As they marched across Bosnia, Serbian troops rounded up local Muslims and systematically gunned them down in scenes reminiscent of Nazi Germany in the 1940s. More than 200,000 Muslims were killed, and 2 million were made refugees.

In China, Mao Zedong's Cultural Revolution was launched in 1966 and continued until his death in 1976.[10] Intended to recapture the revolutionary spirit of China, it became a purge of Mao's enemies and others caught up in the violence. A series of slaughters killed hundreds of thousands and left between 1.6 million and 3 million refugees.

Joseph Stalin was every bit the equal of Mao and Adolf Hitler when it came to mass murder.[11] Stalin's preferred weapon was starvation. His collectivization of Ukraine's family farms in 1930 created a two-year man-made famine known as the Holodomor. Five million Ukrainians died of hunger.

---

8  www.un.org/en/preventgenocide/rwanda/historical-background.shtml.
9  www.ushmm.org/genocide-prevention/countries/bosnia-herzegovina.
10  www.heritage.org/china/commentary/the-legacy-mao-zedong-mass-murder.
11  news.stanford.edu/stories/2010/09/naimark-stalin-genocide-092310.

During and after World War I, the fading Ottoman Empire feared a rebellion by the Armenian people and set about to stop it through forced death marches into the Syrian desert, where Turkish soldiers robbed, raped, and slaughtered them. More than 1 million Armenians were killed, and 200,000 ended up in concentration camps.[12]

Among the most ruthless genocides of all time took place on American soil.[13] When European colonists arrived in North America, this land was home to an estimated 5 million Indigenous people. By the end of the Indian Wars in the late 19th century, fewer than 250,000 were left. Most perished from introduced diseases and brutal massacres.

These genocidal movements, and others, share in common the steps that lead from hatred to the level of dehumanization that allows human beings to carry out atrocities against their fellow man. Countering incivility here and blocking its destructive progression will require an intentional effort by all those who believe there is a better course for America.

"The constant fearmongering in our political discourse unfortunately works," Mayerfeld says. "We have to do actual work to go in the opposite direction.

"There is a positive approach Americans can take to start to reverse this. We don't have to wallow in it. There are actual things we can do, and it starts with individuals behaving differently. Caring for people who are not like you. Having conversations with people who are not like you. Being welcoming to new ideas. Being respectful."

Those are the tenets of our work to promote civility. We are joining others across the country in spreading that message with the hope that it broadly takes hold.

---

12 www.genocide-museum.am/eng/armenian_genocide.php.
13 www.se.edu/native-american/wp-content/uploads/sites/49/2019/09/A-NAS-2017-Proceedings-Smith.pdf.

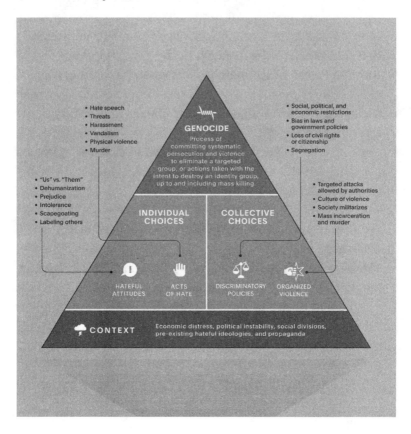

## Social Media

Social media debuted with a bold promise: it would connect distant and disparate people into communities of shared interests, enhance opportunities for conversation, and strengthen interpersonal relationships. No longer would friendships fade and family ties weaken because of distance or a lack of regular contact.

Online and mobile sites would make keeping up to date and in touch effortless and would encourage vigorous debate and the constant sharing of ideas and information. Isolation would be a worry of the past. Borders would disappear as we engaged across

# The Causes and Effects of Incivility    43

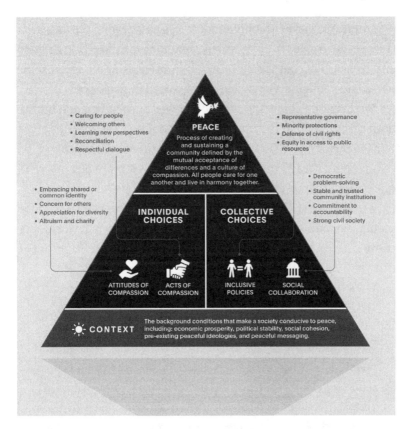

political, cultural, and racial lines to gain a deeper understanding of the world and its people. We would have a tool with which to come together to address issues that had kept us apart.

That was the promise.

The reality, 20 years after Myspace began the great transformation to communicating with our thumbs instead of our tongues, is quite different. Social media has provided a much more efficient platform for the escalation of our divisions. It seems there is no such thing anymore as a minor offense. Everything's a big deal, and we are programmed to fly off the handle at the most minor slight.

Online platforms amplify small voices well beyond the influence they've had in the past or perhaps should have today. There's good and bad in that, but it's certainly disruptive. And it's given some ideas and some individuals an exaggerated importance.

We disagree about the role and power of social media, but we both recognize that it is merely a new tool that reflects old problems in our society. This is the first mode of mass communication that is controlled by individuals. That makes it more of a mirror of our culture than previous iterations of mass media.

As with most things, we sharply disagree on whether social media has had a positive or negative impact on our world, our communities, and our well-being as well as its potential for the future.

Let's hear from Nolan first about social media:

> I suspect part of our difference on this issue is generational as well as reflective of our individual personalities. I was already middle-aged when social media stormed onto the scene. I'd lost touch with most of the people I'd known in my youth and wasn't all that motivated to reconnect. I've always done fine with just a small circle of friends, and even with most of those, I didn't feel a need to touch base every day.
>
> Steve is far more social. He makes friends easily and works to nurture those friendships. I think he went to school with everyone in Detroit and much of Michigan, and he maintains friendships for years and decades.
>
> I'll admit, I did love my BlackBerry, and I enjoy watching funny animal videos on Instagram. But I lost my Facebook password a few years ago and haven't bothered to create a new one. My text messages and X posts tend to be on the terse side, often just one or two words. I haven't mastered the OMG/LOL shorthand, and my lack of digital dexterity makes carrying on a conversation by text excruciating.

My real concern, however, is that social media has never made good on its original promise to be a unifying force and, instead, serves as an instrument of division and incivility.

We were naïve to believe a more efficient and universal means of communication would foster understanding and make our interactions more civil. Instead, what's become more efficient is our ability to bully, insult, and distort.

Rather than bringing us out of our shells, too many of us have withdrawn into a world where most of our contact with other people takes place in the digital space. Face-to-face encounters have become less frequent. For a younger generation, that means they are harder to navigate, since they have so little experience with real-time, in-person interactions.

Instead of contributing to our collective intellectual and emotional growth, social media has brought out the worst in us. It's particularly detrimental to the young.

Research.com says that 37 percent of middle school and high school students report having been cyberbullied, and 90 percent say online harassment has had a negative impact on themselves and their peers.

And unlike the bullying of my youth, which took place in person, at school or on the playground, and usually faded over time, online harassment is not a problem people age out of. Sixty-one percent of adult Americans say they've been bullied online.

Social media posts are too often used to belittle and silence those who disagree with us. Instead of encouraging respectful debate, the confrontational tactics so prevalent on social media serve to shut down conversations.

Let's just say, social media has not been good for the cause of civility. As the technology becomes more sophisticated, the opportunities for exploiting it for harm multiply.

Human nature, I guess, demands that an invention created to improve the spread of information will ultimately become just as adept at spewing misinformation. Those who find an advantage in keeping the public misinformed and fearful are using social media platforms as a powerful weapon.

The Pew Research Center reports that 19 percent of American adults get their news primarily from social media sites, while 29 percent still rely on traditional news sources such as newspapers and their websites.[14] That gives social media considerable influence on public opinion.

It used to be that joining the community of news providers required a significant investment. Newspapers needed printing presses, buildings, and a large staff of trained professionals in circulation, advertising, and editorial departments. Television and radio stations required expensive equipment and personnel along with a license from the federal government before they could transmit their product to a mass audience.

Today the cost of entry into the news business is much lower. A computer connected to a server is about all that's required to set yourself up as a "journalist." Frankly, you might even get away with just a smartphone.

So the hierarchy of credibility is much less clear. An article posted by a long-established news outlet appears in a web search on the same screen as the ramblings of Bob the Blogger operating out of his mother's basement.

News consumers must be more discerning and work much harder to find information sources they can trust. That's particularly urgent with the emergence of more sophisticated technology, including artificial intelligence (AI).

Over the past decade, using the web to spread misinformation and propaganda has become an established tactic in American politics. It's now part of the strategic planning of most campaigns. These efforts, often funded clandestinely by the campaigns

---

[14] https://www.pewresearch.org/journalism/fact-sheet/social-media-and-news-fact-sheet/.

themselves, plant rumors and lies on websites that are quickly spread by social media users.

One of the more notorious examples is 2016's "Pizzagate" episode. The conspiracy theory claimed that the New York City Police Department had discovered evidence of a pedophile ring linked to officials of the Democratic Party while searching a laptop belonging to disgraced former congressman Anthony Weiner.

The human trafficking and child sex operation supposedly operated out of a pizzeria in Washington, DC. Although it was immediately discredited by the police department, the false report went viral on social media. Who knows how many voters went to the polls believing it was true?

That effort at deceiving voters pales in comparison to what's now possible from mischief makers armed with AI. Like social media, AI has the potential to be incredibly useful, but also like social media, this technology is frightening when considered for its ability to distort reality. Videos can be created that literally put words in a candidate's mouth, and in his or her own voice, that were never spoken.

The public won't be able to believe their own ears or eyes. Can any democracy survive such a high-level manipulation of the truth? Only if the electorate commits to not allowing itself to be divided by lies and fearmongering.

Steve shares a concern about social media's negative characteristics and its potential for harm. But he is more optimistic about its potential to mature into a medium whose benefits outweigh its risks. Let's hear from him.

I have to start this section with a confession: scrolling through social media has become an almost singular obsession for me—especially on workdays. It's true to the point that everyone around me knows, is annoyed by it, and probably they've had it with me and the distraction that interrupts everything from casual coffee meetings to very serious discussions.

The phone, and the social media on it, are the first things on my mind when I wake up and the last when I finally go to sleep at night for one reason: the ease of aggregated, broadly rendered information.

On a platform like Twitter/X, for instance, I can get vital information about what's going on in Detroit, where I live; in Baltimore and Chicago and Lexington, Kentucky, cities where I have lived; and tailored content about every issue I write or care about.

One of my favorite feeds is an account called Historic Vids, which posts videos from the past that contain revelatory or surprising information. A recent video chronicled the evolution of typewriters from the late 1800s up through the 1950s. Another featured former president Gerald Ford in 1989 explaining how he thought the first woman might be elected president in our country.

I can jump right from that to the latest news headlines, sports scores, or great cooking ideas. Can you name another way to do that with something that fits in the palm of my hand and is available 24/7?

In my lifetime, the spread of information, and its instant availability, represents the single biggest change in the way we live.

But that doesn't mean it's without its foibles.

The way I use social media reflects my sensibilities—information-hungry, curious, quirky. But it could just as easily reflect those sensibilities if they were vile or prurient, or if my aim was to engage in dismissive and disrespectful political and cultural conversation.

Sadly, social media reflects us—the users and the culture we live in—rather than who we might want or need to be.

As easily as it opens up the world, it can be used to create funnels of information that sort out anything that might contradict or challenge our own ideas about something. The same goes for people: if someone doesn't conform to our outlook or opinions, we can quickly push them out of our social media circles.

All the tools essentially encourage this. You can mute someone. Block them. Unfriend them. And of course, it's not enough just to do it, to expel someone from your circle—you have to announce it to everyone else for the quick and ardent support that causes a rush of adrenaline. "I blocked so-and-so; I'll never speak to them again!" And everyone else cheers.

Social media has become an easy weapon for those hoping to spread lies or other forms of misinformation. Things spread so quickly on social media that a falsehood can become a truism almost instantly. In politics, of course, this helps embed misunderstandings and conspiracy theories into the bedrock of our discourse so that honest debate takes a back seat to endless fact-checking and the refuting of falsehoods.

In those ways, social media reflects—and to some extent, encourages—our worst instincts and behaviors. Especially for young people, it is teaching us all the wrong things: that the world is about the exclusion of counterideas and that we should expel them with all the hostility and anger we possibly can.

So what should we do? Social media is a huge part of my life and a critical source of information for me. But it's also a scourge on the kind of civil discourse and exchange that I want to encourage. I believe we must all be patient.

Social media is really in its infancy, at least with regard to its place as a central mode of communication. It's only been a decade, maybe a bit longer, since social media became dominant in the public discourse. If we look back at the infancy of nearly every form of communication, we'll find an equally troubled beginning.

Take the telegraph, for instance, which was used to master effect in the run-up to and beginning of the Civil War, as a means for propaganda and lies. Civil War historian Yael Sternhell, writing in the *New York Times* in 2013, recounted how a newspaper in Richmond, Virginia, decried the telegraph's use—in 1863. "It covers us all over with lies, fills the very air we breathe and obscures the very sun," the newspaper's editors wrote. "[It] makes us doubt everything we read, because we know that the chances are ten to one it is false."

Many people have said the same about social media.

By World War I and, certainly, by World War II, the telegraph had become an indispensable tool—not just for the fast spread of information but for communications among troops and leaders managing the wars. In other words, the medium grew up as the culture adapted to its presence and use, and the kinks were worked out.

You could tell similar stories about the early days of radio, television, and nearly every other technological advance in communications. Early on, they were troubled reflections of deep problems in our culture. Later, they became vital parts of our communications arsenal. We wouldn't imagine a world without any of them.

My hopes for social media run along the same trajectory. As it matures, the culture will adapt to it and lean more toward its potential and power for effective, fast, and truthful communication. Meanwhile, we all must acknowledge its drawbacks and, if we're enthusiasts, recognize the difference between what happens on social media and what should be happening in the real world.

We don't have to quit social media to know how damaging it can be to civil discourse. But we must commit to backing away from the attitudes and behaviors that social media is teaching us and embrace almost the opposite way of interacting with each other to achieve civil, reasonable outcomes in our interpersonal relationships and exchanges.

In the next chapter, we'll look at how we can move away from incivility.

## Chapter Insights

- A thriving democratic government stresses consensus building and compromise that takes into account the needs and concerns of the minority party.
- When debating or arguing, remember that neither side gets everything it wants, but everyone gets something.
- Diversity of views isn't tolerated in Congress these days, and dissenters are driven out.
- 80 percent of Americans believe their representatives are most responsive to their large financial backers.
- Research has found that anger evoked by attack ads is more influential than any other emotion that motivates voters.
- Unfortunately, civics classes are de-emphasized in favor of STEM . . . and nearly 33 percent of Americans cannot name the three branches of government.
- The federal government spends $50 per student for STEM education and only $0.05 per student on civics.
- 61 percent of adult Americans say they've been bullied online.

## Recommended Actions

- Broaden your information sources beyond social media.
- Engage intentionally with those who are not like you.
- Avoid the incivility traps on social media.
- Be respectful in all communications.

---

### QUESTIONS FOR YOU

How do your early experiences align or contrast with your current beliefs?

Is there a religious influence on your politics? If so, describe it.

Is there an educational influence on your politics? If so, describe it.

Is there a regional influence on your politics? If so, describe it.

Is there an industrial or career influence on your politics? If so, describe it.

Looking at these influences, what feelings arise? Are you glad to see this influence on your beliefs or surprised? How might that change your thinking going forward?

# 3

# The Four Pillars of Civility

We are an angry nation. Our disagreements have ripped us apart, made us suspicious of each other, and created a widespread sense that there is no path back to a more civil society.

Incivility has become endemic, a plague that has destroyed productive dialogue and made honest, meaningful conversations too rare. Instead, we have noise. We shout past each other without ever hearing what's being said.

Increasingly, our preference is for engagement that affirms our viewpoints rather than challenges them. We've become too content to live in echo chambers, surrounded by others who mirror our beliefs and behaviors.

Instead of viewing our political parties as two parts of a whole, essential to one another despite their different values, we see them as two armies competing for total dominance. This is producing a win-at-all-costs culture, where the objective of so many arguments and so many political exchanges is to shut down the other side. That's not a reasonable expectation.

The solution: Encourage people to engage in civil conversation with the goal of gaining an understanding that builds respect, breaks down walls, and chases away the fear that leads to hate.

Sounds easy, but there's nothing simple about it. We can't seem to get to that first step: talking to each other. The Pew Research

Center reveals that roughly 60 percent of Americans find it too stressful to talk politics with those with whom they disagree.

So they just don't. They either avoid discussing difficult political and cultural issues or sidestep engaging with one another altogether. And our nation's giant chasm grows wider.

That's not OK.

Incivility is destroying our communities and our families. If left unchecked, it has the potential to topple our country. If you find that an overstatement, think about the last time one of our political bodies saw Republicans and Democrats coming together to solve a difficult problem. It rarely happens these days. And that's a symptom of the breakdown in civil discourse.

We are also well schooled in assertiveness, convinced we must answer every slight. We feel obliged to respond when someone says something that offends us. Holding our tongues is a lost art.

Remember the famous scene in Roger Rabbit where the bad guys are searching for Roger, who is hiding in a cabinet? They walk through the room tapping out the opening cadence to "Shave and a Haircut." It finally becomes too much for Roger, who bursts out from his hiding place to blurt out "Two bits!" Like the rabbit, we can't help ourselves. We feel the need to express our views no matter how hurtful or inappropriate.

In our presentations, we urge our audiences to follow the advice passed along by someone we trust before offering an opinion, either verbally or in writing. Ask yourself three questions:

- Does this need to be said?
- Does it need to be said right now?
- And does it need to be said by me?

Keep those questions taped to your screen, and it may prevent you from sending out words that can destroy your reputation or career, or worse, your relationships. Learning when a response is warranted and when silence is the better tool is critical to living a civil life.

And yet there are times when a forceful answer is indeed warranted and when anger is appropriate. What we've been doing over the past few years is contemplating how the two of us, who disagree as passionately as any two people in America, can confront each other in robust and often heated debates while maintaining an unbreakable friendship.

No one would mistake either one of us for Mahatma Gandhi. We lose our tempers. We get angry. We are still both working on patience and self-control. But we also understand the need to keep striving to do better. The commitment to civility is not just a courtesy; it's a basic ingredient to fostering healthy relationships and maintaining communities that are able to address challenges. Civility is the cornerstone of both a cohesive society and lasting friendships.

So how do we get there?

We have settled on four pillars of civility that help us on a personal level and, we believe, will tone down the hostility in even the tensest environments.

First is **dropping assumptions** and forgetting what we think we know about the people with whom we disagree. Instead, we seek to fill information gaps with knowledge gained through personal interactions.

Second is **setting honest goals** for those conversations. If your objective going into a discussion is to beat the other person into the ground with the superiority of your intellect, forget about it. A conversation is not a competition and should not be treated as a win/lose proposition. The only legitimate motive for a discussion is to learn something about an issue or a person that you didn't know when the talking began.

That requires **practicing active listening**, which is the third pillar. Too often we hear a person's voice, but we don't digest what they are saying because we are lost in our own thoughts or plotting our responses. Active listening is an art that must be learned and practiced, and it depends on having confidence that you will get your turn to reply.

The fourth pillar is to **keep coming back** to the conversation. Civility-building doesn't happen overnight. Watch some of our TV clips, and you'll too often see two grown men going after each other full-on. Some of them even make us cringe. But no matter how hot the argument gets, we never resort to name-calling or personal insults. We are mindful that words can be deadly weapons. The commitment to never go personal allows us to walk away, cool down, and come back another day to pick up where we left off.

In subsequent chapters, we will go into more detail about these pillars and how you can lean on them to live a more civil life and bring civility to your relationships. Once you understand the pillars, the next step is putting them into action. When we present Civility Sessions, we ask the audience to break into small groups and practice the principles we discussed.

Sometimes, participants are grouped with friends or coworkers, sometimes with strangers. Their assignment is to share their stories, to put on the table the values and experiences that have made them who they are.

The conversations usually get off to an awkward start. We've been conditioned to avoid certain subjects, politics chief among them. And we can't deny the risk that comes with candid conversations. Make a mistake, use the wrong word, touch a taboo subject, and it can ruin your life or get you canceled.

But it is surprising how quickly our audiences move beyond apprehension and start not only talking about themselves but asking questions of their tablemates. Most often, they aren't ready to stop talking when the timer goes off, no matter how long we give them. And they can't wait to go back for more.

This exercise isn't just for strangers. This approach can benefit coworkers, friends, and family members who have long-standing relationships and think they know everything there is to know about each other. The chances are good that you don't have much idea about how or why the people close to you believe what they do.

In one of our early sessions, we paired two suburban women who were neighbors and friends. They had walked together nearly every morning for nine years. One voted mostly for Democrats and the other mostly for Republicans. They knew that much about each other, but they had no clue as to why. They had intentionally avoided talking about politics out of fear of jeopardizing their friendship.

During their breakout discussion, they learned there were specific reasons for how each voted, reasons rooted in personal experiences that shaped their political perspectives. They didn't reach any sort of agreement during that discussion; that wasn't the point. But they did lift a barrier that had inhibited their friendship.

"We don't have to walk on eggshells anymore," one of the women said when they returned to the session.

You may be asking, Why go to the trouble of learning to nurture a relationship across political divides? Allow us to answer that question with a story about a young woman we encountered while doing a Civility Session for a nonprofit group in Lansing, Michigan.

While we were speaking, she sat at the front of the audience, furiously taking notes. When we finished, she waited patiently until the crowd had cleared before approaching us. She had a problem she wanted to discuss. She was newly married, and she and her husband wanted to start a family.

But she was worried about an unhealthy family dynamic. Her husband and her father disagreed bitterly about politics. And they couldn't seem to talk about anything else. Whenever they were together, their conversations turned into angry arguments they couldn't move past. Inevitably, harsh words led to long periods of silence and separation. Worse, they had convinced themselves they hated each other and were no longer interested in trying to fix what was broken.

"I don't want to bring a child into this environment," she told us, tears welling in her eyes. "I want my child to be loved by people who love each other."

We advised her to invite them to engage in the exercises we describe in our presentation and detail in this book. She was skeptical it would help or even if they would agree to try. We could tell she was looking for more from us, a better answer. So we tossed aside our notes and asked her to present her husband and father-in-law with some soul-searching questions:

> Why are your politics more important than maintaining the healthy father/son relationship you both once valued?
>
> In those dark hours when you need the people who love you, will it matter who's a Republican and who's a Democrat?
>
> Why is it so vital for you to prevail in this ongoing dispute?
>
> What will winning the argument bring you?

Neither man will decide the outcome of any election. Neither will determine the direction of government policy. They can't change the world. But they can change their own relationship and hugely impact their family—possibly for generations. If they were willing to put their love for one another ahead of their politics, it would enrich their lives and that of their future children and grandchildren.

Isn't that what matters? When faced with intractable differences with someone you care about, ask yourself the questions we suggested the young woman present to her loved ones. Don't be obsessed with changing the other person's views. Decide to value the relationship more than the dispute.

Disagreement need not lead to painful division. That's what we believe and what we try to live. Doing so hasn't brought us any nearer to agreement. But that was never our goal. It's not important to us that we share the same opinion. That's not where we find the benefit in the relationship. Rather, our willingness to debate across the divide forces us to vigorously defend our individual opinions, a process that makes those viewpoints sharper and more intellectually rooted.

This is the principle that drives the Civility Project—a deeply held belief that there is value in engaging with people who hold different views and have lived different experiences. Embracing empathy and respect for "the other side" doesn't mean abandoning your own convictions. Rather, it tamps down the resentment and suspicion that too often causes us to isolate ourselves from others and grow fearful of another position.

In essence, we're working toward the transformation of hostile discourse into respectful dialogue—toward a society where differing opinions are acknowledged, understood, and engaged with civility and compassion.

Throughout history, our nation has weathered divisions, from the strife of the Civil War to the reckoning of the civil rights movements, and many, many others. Yet the present moment has a different feel. A Great Unraveling is afoot, a coming apart that portends a dangerous future for America if left unaddressed. The work we undertake here is rooted in the belief that change can start at the grassroots level in the conversations we have with neighbors, family, and friends.

It's not a panacea for the grand challenges our nation faces, but it's a vital step—an investment in the power of dialogue and understanding. We are optimistic about the potential for change, one civil conversation at a time. But we aren't Pollyannaish. The current state of the world is undeniably overwhelming. We often feel helpless. And so we lash out, dig in, erect barriers. And there are fewer places of refuge. We've witnessed a gradual erosion of the civil institutions that once provided a sense of community.

Fifty years ago, nearly everybody went to church or temple.[1] There were civic organizations that fostered cohesiveness and a shared purpose. They brought us together in communities with common missions. Those service organizations are fading away and houses of worship are struggling to fill their pews.

There are fewer organizations that bring us together and connect us to our communities, and so we lose our sense of responsibility for taking care of each other. We are more transient; it is far more rare than it once was for people to spend their whole lives in one place. We are less likely to know everyone in our city or even on our block. That anonymity reduces the consequences of incivility, and so it becomes easier to forget our manners, to care less about who we offend.

Complicating our ability to come together is the reality that the prevalent political narratives encourage discord rather than understanding. Social media, a tool that was supposed to connect us, instead rewards the most hateful confrontations. The rise of cable TV news programs and the rabidly partisan nature of our politics also fuel our fear and mistrust of each other.

We must resist falling into that trap. We don't pretend it's easy or that it comes naturally to us; we must be constantly vigilant about our commitment to civil engagement.

## Chapter Insights

- Holding our tongues is a lost art.
- The commitment to civility is not just a courtesy; it's a basic ingredient to fostering healthy relationships and maintaining communities that are able to address challenges.

---

1 news.gallup.com/poll/341963/church-membership-falls-below-majority-first-time.aspx.

- A conversation is *not* a competition.
- Active listening is an art that must be learned and practiced, and it depends on having confidence that you will get your turn to reply.

## Recommended Actions

- Encourage people—family, friends, colleagues—to engage in a civil discussion to gain an understanding that builds respect, breaks down walls, and chases away the fear that leads to hate.
- Remember, the chances are good that you don't have much idea about how or why the people close to you believe what they do, so listen to their viewpoints to better understand their position.

---

### QUESTIONS FOR YOU

To prepare for civility-building with people who hold different perspectives from you, consider the following questions:

How did you come to your beliefs or political leanings? What experiences, values, and teachings in your life led you to your beliefs today?

Why do you want to have civil conversations with people who believe or vote differently from you? What outcomes do you hope to achieve with these conversations?

Do you know of anyone who already does this well? If so, what positions them to practice civility? What could you learn from them?

# 4

# Pillar 1

## Dropping Assumptions

There's an old saying in the newspaper business: "When you assume, you make an ass of you and me."

There is no substitute for facts. No shortcut to bypass careful research. No tool better than information. What you think you know will get you in trouble.

Often, when we meet people we disagree with, we jump to all sorts of conclusions about who they are, what they believe, and what motivates them. In *The Civility Project*, we talk about resisting the instinct to do that and, instead, taking active steps to fill the information gaps with knowledge. In other words, do the reporting before you start drawing conclusions.

We ask people to sit down together and attempt a productive, civil conversation and to start by wiping the slate clean. Forget what you think you know about another person and why they believe the things they do; it's probably wrong—or at the very least, incomplete.

Do the reporting. Get the facts. Fill in the information gaps with knowledge. Don't fall back on stereotypes and guesswork.

A core principle of civility is that all good people come to their opinions in the same way: they take the available information, run it through the filter of their personal experiences and values, and form a point of view. If that viewpoint differs from yours, it doesn't make them stupid or their opinions invalid.

Taking the time to understand those values and experiences is key to building the respect necessary for civil engagement. It may not lead to agreement or even a softening of positions. But hopefully it will enable honest conversations that bust through the assumptions that lead to fear and hate.

And that's the real problem. We assume we hate people based on what we know about their politics, their skin color, or where they come from. We choose to avoid rather than to engage. It makes it easier to be rude, accusatory, mean.

Unfortunately, incivility is a ticket to success in today's world. Social media rewards the loudest, harshest voices, which garner the most friends and likes, though there's nothing friendly or likable about their nasty narratives.

Americans once were far more skilled in engaging in civil conversation with those who held opposing viewpoints. But today, many Americans believe they can't have relationships with people whose politics are different. Many even avoid family get-togethers and holiday celebrations for fear that their political disagreements will fume across the table.

Assumptions enable us to avoid the hard work of actually getting to know another person. We rely on preconceptions to assign labels and descriptors, which is lazy and dangerous.

We hear words such as *progressive* or *conservative*, *Republican* or *Democrat*, *Christian* or *Muslim* or *Jew*, *Black* or *White* or *Brown*, and our brain spits out a profile that may have nothing to do with who someone is as a complete person.

Not having that full picture makes it easy to assign negative motives for why someone identifies with one group or another. It's an easy way out and one that serves as a convenient filter to screen from our lives those who make us uncomfortable.

It encourages us to look at those who hold different views, operate under a different set of principles, as inferior. We see them as less than us in their value as people. In our minds, they're not as good and thus not worthy of our time or attention—or worse, not entitled to the same rights and privileges that we enjoy.

There are real dangers to that on both a macro and a micro level. Politically, we've seen the consequences of marginalizing large swaths of people whose views we disdain. They tend to push back in ways that might not be in their best interests, let alone the nation's, but that make them feel empowered.

The attitude reflected in Barack Obama's derisive remark about Americans who "cling to their guns and religion," Hillary Clinton's "basket of deplorables" comment, and Joe Biden's "garbage" depiction explains part of the reason those voters flocked to Donald Trump in 2016 and again in 2024. Obama, Clinton, and Biden were making assumptions about voters they had ignored or had never bothered trying to understand. And look at the result.

This is playing out more often in our politics. The politicians who rise to power assign negative characteristics to those who voted against them, completely dismissing their concerns and desires. One side foists all the blame for the nation's ills on the other. Political strategists have determined that demonizing the other party rather than engaging in informed debate is a sure route to victory. It's not enough to win; the objective is to destroy the opponent in the process and to do so by any means necessary.

Plus, knowing that if your side loses, it will be completely shut out of the governing process places a much greater urgency on winning.

On an interpersonal level, our assumptions are the bunkers that protect us from the discomfort of being challenged, of having to defend our own values and beliefs to those who frighten us.

A State Policy Network poll from April 2023 found that in the previous year, 59 percent of Americans had stayed quiet about their political views to avoid conflicts.[1] That's not a recipe for bringing us closer together as a people, and certainly not for encouraging the

---

[1] https://spn.org/articles/polling-spotlight-politics-is-an-afterthought/.

productive debate necessary to reach consensus on how to meet the many difficult challenges we face.

We wrote earlier about the two women who were walking buddies for years but were afraid to talk politics. As it turns out, one of the friends had experienced a difficult financial stretch early in her marriage. Her family struggled, and she blamed it on the government policies that were in place at the time. That shaped her political worldview and led her to favor one party over the other. Her preferences were based on personal experience, not on sinister influences or a lack of information. Once she talked about what she had gone through with her friend, they could walk together without walking on eggshells. Knowledge enabled them to speak more freely and with less suspicion.

In our Civility Sessions, we encourage people to engage in conversations aimed at drawing out the experiences and values that make individuals who they are and inform their beliefs.

During the COVID-19 pandemic, one of the great divides was between those who embraced vaccinations and those who refused them, oftentimes at the risk of being ostracized in their communities. Many of us assumed those who rejected the shots were motivated by superstition, misinformation, or a skewed political allegiance.

But did we ask them their reasons before judging them? Perhaps they had legitimate concerns about the impact of the vaccine. Maybe they had past experiences that influenced their decision. Or it may well be they were superstitious, misinformed, or politically slanted. But there was no way of knowing without asking. Without that information, the tendency was to dismiss the concerns of the vaccine objectors as entirely without merit. Vaccines, then, became a major wedge at a time when the country needed to hold together, and everybody thought the other side was literally out to get them.

The best way to begin any relationship with someone from a different background or whose political views don't align with yours is by asking questions intended to build the knowledge necessary to supplant assumptions.

It's a beneficial exercise even among close friends and family members who assume they know all there is to know about each other. We did this ourselves many years into our friendship when National Public Radio's StoryCorps project came to Detroit.[2]

StoryCorps is an NPR project that travels the country collecting American stories about relationships. They park a Winnebago in a city and invite people to come down with someone they know, sit across a table with a microphone between them, and record their "story." How do they know each other? What is the nature of their relationship? What are its highlights and challenges?

For most people, this is a chance to clear the air with a family member or a spouse. But as soon as StoryCorps announced it was coming to Detroit, Stephen thought of someone else he'd like to take with him: Nolan.

The two had been friends and had been working together for about 10 years at that point. They knew each other well and had worked out the early kinks in their relationship. They didn't take cheap shots at each other during arguments or resort to insults or name-calling. And they valued each other—as friends and as colleagues.

On the way to the Detroit Institute of Arts, where the StoryCorps Winnebago was parked, Stephen explained to Nolan what was on his mind.

He said that this wouldn't be a regular back-and-forth between them—an argument or even a discussion about the differences in their points of view. Instead, Stephen said, they were going to go into this small space and tell each other their stories. Nolan would tell Stephen why he's a conservative—what experiences he

---

[2] Here is the link to listen to that interview if you're interested: wdet.org/2017/08/16/StoryCorps-Detroit-Podcast-A-Tale-of-Two-Papers-Opinions/.

had and the things that he'd learned over time that told him that conservatism was the right way to solve policy issues and problems.

And then Stephen would return the favor. He'd explain to Nolan the path he took to progressivism, the things that suggest to him that that's the right prism for resolving public policy.

Each took care to be as detailed and intentional in their explanations as possible. When they were done, three things—most of them surprising—had happened.

First, they both learned things they hadn't known about the other. Despite having been friends and working together for nearly a decade, there were just a lot of details they hadn't yet divulged about themselves. Things about their childhoods, their educations, the experiences they'd had that had a real influence on the way they came to see the world.

The second thing that happened was more startling: both men heard things from the other that they recognized in themselves. It was mostly aspirations and dreams they shared—about their families, about the nation, and about humanity. It was the first time they realized that despite their profound differences in politics and policy, in many instances, they really wanted the same outcomes: prosperity and opportunity, fairness, a sense that good fortune would be plentiful in the future.

The third thing that came out of Stephen and Nolan's StoryCorps discussion was a change in the way they interacted with each other going forward. They continued to argue—always passionately and sometimes even angrily. But because they knew much more about each other and had learned about the values and beliefs they shared, their discussions adopted a great deal more understanding and leeway. Ever since, they've been slower to judge each other harshly and slower to jump on one another in disagreements.

They think a lot about the timing of that StoryCorps discussion—some 10 years into knowing each other—and wonder how different things between them might have gone if they'd started off with that exchange. What if they'd actually gotten to know each other—really know a lot about each other—before they ever had a discussion or an argument?

Or is it even possible to have such an open and far-reaching conversation at the outset of a relationship? Do we need the time to grow into a friendship, to feel safe enough to explore our deepest thoughts and yearnings? Regardless, this proves that you can never know a person as well as you think you do, which is why making assumptions never serves anyone.

We have attained a level of confidence in our relationship that enables us to discuss the most difficult issues, including race, with full candor and the confidence that it won't break our friendship.

We began this book with the story about Steve's encounter with the two women on Mackinac Island who were convinced they hated him because they were offended by the things he'd written. Many of us are guilty of doing the same thing. We say "I hate that person" simply because he or she has said or written something with which we disagree. Defaulting to hating our political opponents is an instinct driven by assumptions.

The women assumed certain things about Stephen that were softened by his willingness to listen to their concerns. He, too, walked away with greater empathy for how their families were impacted by the policies he supported.

Coming to mutual respect didn't require that he or they change their positions. They were no closer to agreement when the conversation ended than when it began. They walked away still disagreeing, but no longer hating, because they were willing to take the risk of hearing each other out.

Knowing what others have experienced and how it has impacted them tempers the tendency to make knee-jerk judgments or dismiss another's opinion as invalid. Drop your assumptions and sit across from another person in a spirit of curiosity and with the eagerness to learn the things about them you don't know. And with a willingness to show them who you are.

It's much more difficult to feel ill will toward someone once you know their story and have told them yours.

## Chapter Insights

- Forget what you think you know about another person and why they believe the things they do; it's probably wrong—or at the very least, incomplete.
- A core principle of civility is that all good people come to their opinions in the same way: they take the available information, run it through a filter of their personal experiences and values, and form a point of view.
- A State Policy Network poll from April 2023 found that in the previous year, 59 percent of Americans had stayed quiet about their political views to avoid conflicts.

## Recommended Actions

- Do the reporting. Get the facts. Fill in the information gaps with knowledge. Don't fall back on stereotypes and guesswork.
- Begin any relationship with someone from a different background or whose political views don't align with yours by asking questions intended to build the knowledge necessary to supplant assumptions.
- Get to know others—really know a lot about each other—before having a political discussion or argument.

---

### QUESTIONS FOR YOU

As you prepare to embrace the pillar of dropping assumptions, you might want to examine what assumptions you hold toward people with different political views. These questions can help you explore preconceived notions and find the root of how you came to hold them.

What do you assume about people who support the opposite political party from you? (Be honest! No one will hear your answers—but it's valuable to explore the assumptions we hold to determine if they serve us, or perhaps not.)

Where do these assumptions come from? Did someone in your past believe this and pass these beliefs on to you? Do they come from the media? Somewhere else?

Are these assumptions true? If not, what beliefs might you replace them with?

What is the benefit of holding assumptions about other people and their beliefs?

# 5

# Pillar 2
## Setting Honest Goals

A conversation is not a competition. Keep that truth in mind and civil discussions across even the widest divides are possible.

Too often, we set out in our encounters with someone who holds opposite beliefs with the objective of winning. Our intention is to dismantle the other person with the superiority of our argument. We want to beat them into the ground with the primacy of our intellect and our mastery of the facts.

Sounds like a blast, doesn't it? Only a masochist would voluntarily sit through an hour of that.

And it's not a true conversation. It's an exercise in arrogance, which won't lead to anything productive. Just the opposite, in fact. The desire to win an argument, to convert the other party to your way of thinking, too often leads to frustration and disappointment. Or worse: anger and resentment.

To give interactions the chance to produce benefits, it is vital to set honest goals at the outset. Here's a clue: Winning is not an honest goal. Nor is setting out to convert another to a different way of thinking. First of all, it's rarely possible. We've been arguing with each other for more than 15 years, and we can think of very few examples where either of us has changed the other's mind on anything of substance. If we suddenly found ourselves in total agreement, go ahead and pack us off to the undertaker.

Conversion conversations are not only unproductive; they're not much fun. No one wants to listen to a sermon. Lecturing your conversation partner is the poorest way to get your point across.

What it most often accomplishes is the silencing of the other person. The more you preach, the more they shut down. And that's where we are today in America. Pew Research finds that almost half of Americans have stopped talking about politics. It's just not pleasant. And it's too loaded with risk.

Why is it important that everyone feels welcome to express their opinions and feel comfortable engaging in back-and-forth discussions on serious issues? Because there are a lot of bad and harmful ideas floating around. They need to be brought to the surface to be debated and discredited.

There are also a lot of people who have something to say but feel ignored. That leads to disenfranchisement. It's vital we talk with each other. But urging people to engage in frank conversations is a difficult request.

Again, the first step is to set an honest goal for the encounter. What do you hope to get out of it? For us, it's never been about scoring points. We aren't out to embarrass each other or to walk away as the victor. And we know the likelihood we will reach an agreement is slim.

Yet we keep talking. Why? Because we find considerable value in our discussions. Our goal, when we sit down to talk, is to learn something we didn't know before. We almost always accomplish that. We also use our conversations as a means of sharpening our own views. We test our arguments against each other with the hope of finding their strengths and weaknesses. So the goals we've set are to learn from each other and to gain a greater understanding of what makes the other tick.

Establish those clear intentions right from the start and then demonstrate a commitment to them by spending at least as much time asking questions as you do expressing your own views. (You'll learn more about this approach in the next chapter on listening.)

That helps create a space for authentic learning and the validation of ideas instead of building a battlefield. Both parties will walk away feeling stimulated instead of bullied and thus much more likely to engage again.

Ultimately, the goal isn't to forcibly change minds but to open them, to create an atmosphere of mutual respect. Through civil conversation, we can encourage an acceptance of the principle that differing opinions can coexist no matter how entrenched or vehement the disagreement.

Once you've decided there's value in engagement, put some ground rules in place to ensure things don't go off-track. Understanding what each participant expects from the exchange and determining their comfort level for contentious conversation are paramount.

Perhaps the most important rule is to check your smugness at the door. One of the most asked questions we get is, "How do you talk to someone who just won't accept the truth?" The answer: you probably can't if you approach the person with that sort of self-righteousness.

We all tend to believe we hold the inviolable truth on a subject and that the facts are all on our side of the table. It's rarely that clear cut. This way of thinking leads to closed ears and closed minds. When we're so convinced we're right, we don't listen to other arguments and believe it is unnecessary to weigh the validity of counterpoints.

Always harbor at least some self-doubt. We've seen too many examples recently of the "absolute" truth changing as new information is uncovered.

It's also important to mind your tone. People know when they're being talked down to. Condescension has no place in a civil conversation.

When thinking about the ground rules, don't forget about taking steps to remove the fear of speaking openly and honestly.

Conversations about difficult issues have always been awkward, especially between people who don't know each other that well.

Today, we also must deal with the reality that such encounters carry the risk of cancellation. In our gotcha culture, it always seems there's someone ready to pounce on every slip of the tongue, every misused word, every unintentional slight.

The danger of shutting down those who misspeak, whether maliciously or accidentally, lies not merely in the act of silencing voices but also in the lost opportunity for growth and learning that stems from open dialogue.

We must take the fear of being canceled out of the equation. Everyone involved in the conversation must agree that it is a safe zone. Intentional insults and hateful comments don't have to be tolerated. But if someone unintentionally offends, use it as a chance to educate rather than condemn. A gentle correction can work to create greater understanding and trust. An overreaction is sure to end the dialogue. Honest conversations will have their share of bumps and bruises. But they pave the way for growth.

Establishing ground rules is crucial to preventing conversations from spiraling into hostility. Discussions about politics obviously can get heated. People are passionate, particularly in this bitter, divisive era. It's OK if the talk gets a little loud.

But don't let it get personal. Keep the language focused on the issue, not on the participants in the conversation.

In all our years of arguing, both in public and in private, we have never let it get personal. We've never allowed things to deteriorate to insults or name-calling, no matter how angry we've become. Not once have we said, "You're a _____."

That's an important boundary and one that should never be crossed. Words can deliver a lasting hurt, and personal attacks are often hard to come back from. When you sense an argument is reaching the point of crossing that line, stop right there and return another day.

It's always OK to walk away temporarily. Change the subject or part to resume at another time. Knowing that the mission is not to convince your conversation partner to change his or her views but rather to exchange ideas and learn something in the process removes some of the pressure.

Vigorous debates with someone who isn't trying to destroy you can actually be stimulating. The intellectual exercise of exchanging informed viewpoints is fun and rewarding.

Such conversations are best started as intentional activities. Give some thought to the right time and place. Both parties must be comfortable. While the civility techniques offered in this book will work to defuse workplace conflicts, political conversations are best held off the job.

The journey to civility requires patience, humility, and an open mind. Civil conversations can break down barriers and reframe perspectives. Setting the stage for such conversation starts well before the talking begins. Setting honest goals, checking your self-righteousness at the door, avoiding personal attacks, and creating cancel-free zones in which to have the conversation will make things go more smoothly.

Following these guidelines has paid dividends for us. Nolan acknowledges his perspectives on America's racial history have undergone a shift, largely influenced by dialogue with Stephen. These discussions unraveled the intricacies of issues such as affirmative action. Hearing their impact from a friend who has lived the experience helps draw a more complete picture.

He also says that, as a pragmatic conservative, lengthy conversations about race with Stephen have moved him toward looking at racism as an economic threat—maintaining a permanent underclass because of inequality is a drain on the economy.

There are still many points of the issue on which we differ, particularly on how to achieve equality. But on this and other subjects, once we recognize we want the same outcome—a fairer, more prosperous society—the arguments over the path to get there become more productive.

## Chapter Insights

- A conversation is not a competition.
- Winning is not an honest goal.
- According to Pew Research, almost 50 percent of Americans have stopped discussing politics.

## Recommended Actions

- The goal of a conversation is to learn something we didn't know before... to learn from each other... and to gain a greater knowledge of what makes the other person tick.
- Establish clear intentions from the start to demonstrate a commitment to them by spending as much time asking questions as you do expressing your own views.
- Check your own smugness at the door.
- Always harbor at least some self-doubt.
- It's also important to mind your tone.
- If someone unintentionally offends, use it as an opportunity to educate rather than condemn.
- Don't let it get personal. Keep the language focused on the issue, not on the participants in the conversation.
- Remember, the journey to civility requires patience, humility, and an open mind.

---

### QUESTIONS FOR YOU

Before you can set honest goals for a conversation with another person, it's important to know what you hope to gain from engaging with others in meaningful and exploratory discussion. Answering these questions might help you understand where you are now and where you'd like to be in the realm of civility-building.

In the past, what have been your reasons for engaging in political discussions with others?

If you've sought to convince someone of your stance, why was that important to you?

If you've sought validation for your beliefs, why did you desire that?

Are you comfortable having a conversation with someone who holds different political beliefs even if the result of that conversation is continued differences? Why or why not?

# 6

# Pillar 3

## Practicing Active Listening

In Old English, the word *listen* means "pay attention to." It's an intentional, purposeful surrender of self-declaration and a leaning in to someone else's thoughts and ideas.

Genuine listening is the third of the four pillars we talk about as keys to civility. Once you are comfortable dropping the assumptions so many of us make about others—based on superficial characteristics like their politics or religion or the place they're from—and once you're comfortable setting realistic, cooperative expectations for your interactions with someone who thinks or believes differently from you, the next step is to listen.

To really listen.

In essence, genuine listening is the bedrock of civil exchange and authentic comprehension across all sorts of divides. It's the fertile ground where seeds of understanding are sown, nurtured by empathy, and grown into robust trees of mutual respect.

It's about curiosity too—truly wanting to know what the other person has to say or what the origins and motivations are for someone's thoughts and beliefs. When we're curious, we're not dismissive; we're open to new ideas, expressions, and experiences.

So how do you do it? How do you actually listen to someone with a genuine investment in what they're saying and trying to communicate? How do you listen deeply and fully with a sense of curiosity and wonder for what the other person is saying?

It's not an easy feat. It requires stepping out of familiar roles, presenting an argument contrary to our convictions. It demands acute attention to and empathy for someone else's thoughts.

This is the first pillar that really asks us to invest, to assign inherent value to the person we are talking with. And that requires a good bit of selflessness, of checking your own certainties and intentions to see the possibilities for learning and understanding through someone else's lens.

Often, even when we believe we are listening to someone, an honest assessment of our activity suggests that's not true, at least not in the way we are describing here. A common mistake is to be too much in our own heads while someone else is trying to communicate their ideas. We think about what we are going to say after the other person stops talking. Each word they utter becomes a building block in our own argument or retort rather than a foundation for understanding their point or rationale.

This is perhaps the most common cause of interruption—the worst form of listening. We get so hyped up about what we want to say in response that we don't even let the other person finish their thought or idea.

Sometimes, we "listen" but judge at the same time. Rather than actually taking what the other person says as a sincere expression of their beliefs or understanding, we are assessing our own measure of what they're saying while they're talking.

Nobody is perfect, and these things are hard to avoid. Even as frequently as we argue, and as long as we've been working at it, we often find ourselves falling into these traps.

It's important to watch for them, though, and when you find yourself interrupting or judging or just waiting for the other person to stop talking, catch yourself, reset, and reinvest in the exchange of ideas.

When we present Civility Sessions, we suggest a few tests to see if you're really listening. The first is simple: listen well enough, and hard enough, that you are able to "mirror" back what the other person said. Maybe not each word but the key points of the other person's remarks.

As a business practice or strategy, this is a popular approach. In an office setting or in a negotiation, there is a supposed strategic advantage to mirroring other people—allies or enemies—for the purpose of winning them over to your side.

The website for the accounting, marketing, and sales tool Intuit, for instance, suggests that showing a level of understanding for a client or adversary gives you a strategic advantage. It disarms the other person and at least gives the impression of investment on your part.

What we are talking about here, though, has a more genuine motive. It's done to gain not a strategic advantage but rather an authentic connection.

Being able to show someone that you've listened to the point that you could authentically repeat their argument goes a long way toward demonstrating actual interest in building a collaborative exchange.

It can disarm, yes. But not in the spirit of "winning." It disarms in the name of showing respect, in the hope that it becomes mutual.

The other test we recommend for true listening is about the response you have to what someone says. Stephen says that when he's really listening to someone and invested in learning more about what they think, he has questions for them when they're done talking. His first instinct, in this listening mode, is not to go immediately to his own thoughts or beliefs but to probe deeper into what the other person is saying.

Maybe they said something you haven't heard before. Maybe they said something you didn't quite catch the full context of or understand how it connects to the point they're making. Or maybe you just want to know more about how they have come to the ideas they hold.

The only way to answer those questions is to ask them to suspend the back-and-forth, just for a bit, and to probe deeper into what someone else really thinks. It requires the confidence that you'll get your turn to offer a retort or explain your position. But the wait is always worth it.

There's an added advantage to asking questions in this way as well. It helps reframe the conversation away from competitive or even combative terms and toward the idea of exchange.

In part, this is just about language. The interrogative sentence, by definition, is probing, not accusatory. It is an admission of both curiosity and the desire for more knowledge—two dynamics that take the edge off conversations. And which are essential to building true civility.

## Chapter Insights

- The word *listen* means "pay attention to." It's an intentional, purposeful surrender of self-declaration and a leaning in to someone else's thoughts and ideas.
- When we're curious, we're not dismissive or shunting. We're open to new ideas, expressions, and experiences.

## Recommended Actions

- While someone else is trying to communicate their ideas, do not use that time to formulate your response. Just listen to them.
- Listen well enough, and hard enough, that you might be able to "mirror" back what the other person said.
- While listening, probe deeper into what the other person is saying.

## QUESTIONS FOR YOU

When we think we're listening, we may actually not be. It takes a lot of effort to embrace the art of listening as outlined in this chapter. If you're willing to do it, it might be worth exploring beforehand how you listen now and identify ways that you can listen better to build civility. These questions will help you explore this topic.

What challenges around listening have you experienced? Have others cut you off so you talk faster to get everything in? Did you grow up in a busy household where it was a competition to be heard? What other listening challenges could have led to your current experience with listening?

Do you know someone who listens well? If so, how does it make you feel when you're in conversation with this person? What might you learn from their listening skills to adopt as your own?

Do you know someone who is a terrible listener? What makes them a bad listener? Can you identify some of their habits to help you avoid doing the same thing in future conversations?

# 7

# Pillar 4
## Keep Coming Back

The aftermath of the 2016 presidential election was a cultural turning point for many reasons, but one change was more noticeable than others. More so than after other elections, which are often contentious and frequently leave at least one side quite bitter, the rancor after 2016 seeped into places far beyond our public interactions. We remember hearing, over and over, from people who felt the cleave that had opened in American politics had begun to swallow their personal lives.

Thanksgiving is always just a few weeks after Election Day in our country, and for many people, it's a kind of temperature check about the results. How did your relatives vote? What did they think of the candidates? How did they feel about the outcomes?

In most years, if any of those questions inspired a dispute, it was a minor argument, a feeble disagreement. But rolling into the 2016 holiday season, people seemed to have heightened and intensified fears about the encounters around the holiday table: "I don't want to see Uncle Joe . . . because I know he voted for the other guy, and I just don't want to talk about it."

How many times were people not just thinking but vocalizing those apprehensions? How many people were opting out of holiday events they went to every year, without fail, because they didn't want to talk about Donald Trump?

That "coming apart" feeling was a major impetus for the Great Lakes Civility Project. As we noticed how much hotter passions were running and how much the country's political strife was beginning to interfere with people's personal lives, their closest-in relationships and spaces, it became clearer than ever that we were losing the ability to talk to one another about our differences.

The assault on family relationships seemed almost novel. Nolan tells a story about that first Thanksgiving after the Trump election when a relative of his burst through the door, late to dinner, and announced, "Nobody talk to me about Donald Trump! I've already been run out of two dinners and this one is my last chance to get something to eat!"

Clearly, we needed something better.

The two of us and our friendship made it through this difficult time nationally without much of a hiccup. It helped that neither of us supported Donald Trump. But beyond the candidate himself, 2016 highlighted some of the fundamental divisions in our politics and culture.

We credit our ease to practice—the pillars that would become the basis for the Civility Project have become the guideposts and touchstones of our interactions. We don't make assumptions about each other, we set reasonable expectations in our exchanges, and we listen actively to each other.

But there's something else we do, routinely and instinctively, that makes the relationship work and gives it staying power. In nearly 20 years of arguing and socializing, neither of us has ever left an argument and said, "I'm done with this guy. I won't be back."

We always return to the table, to the stage, to the bar, to wherever we are having a discussion or argument, over and over. That commitment and dedication allow for disagreement, argument, even bitterness and anger. It's what makes civility possible—the long-term engagement that contextualizes our differences and makes them part of the relationship rather than the foil to it.

It's hard to say when this dynamic took over. At first, back in the mid-2000s when we were just beginning to appear together on television or radio and becoming friends, it was our job to keep coming back. We were in professional positions that brought us into contrapose, and it was work, paid work, to have the discussions we did.

But over time, our commitment to return to the debate between us became a choice more than an obligation. Now it is about investment and personal commitment. We return to the conversation because doing so preserves the ability to show respect and to learn from each other.

Returning to the conversation isn't an admission of defeat; it's an acknowledgment of the depth and breadth of the human experience. It's an investment in empathy, an endeavor to comprehend the person beyond the viewpoint.

Ultimately, the act of returning to these conversations—of persistently seeking to understand—is an act of hope. It's a declaration that despite our differences, there exists a common thread of humanity that binds us all. It's an acknowledgment that amid the turbulence of opposing opinions, there exists an opportunity for connection and progress.

Our families, friends, neighbors, and school or religious communities are precious to us. They are places we already value for things other than political discussion or debate. They form the foundations of our lives, really.

So why would we allow politics to make us walk away from those spaces? How could we? Unfortunately, many Americans have allowed their commitment to their own sense of being right, their own sense of political righteousness, to overshadow their commitment to what's closest to them in the first place.

We also allow politics to get in the way of love. We have come to feel betrayed when a family member or some other loved one takes a different direction politically than the one we choose. We can't countenance their decision-making and fear that facing those family members will intensify our distress.

But family is family for a reason—it's who you turn to in your most troubled circumstances, and for most of us, the people who have to be there no matter what. And if it's not your family, then it's your friends or your neighbors or some community you belong to that you turn to because you know they're always there.

Keying on those relationships and valuing them more than politics is critical to maintaining civility, and it's the primary reason this effort has such importance—the repair of the damage done by incivility to our most precious bonds.

In a society where polarization seems pervasive, these conversations become not a means to bridge divides but a beacon guiding us toward a more tolerant, empathetic, and enlightened future. They offer a glimpse into the humanity that unites us beyond our political affiliations—a reminder that beneath the veneer of opinions lies a shared humanity seeking connection and understanding.

Hence the importance of persistently returning to these conversations, of valuing the depth and breadth they offer. They are not just exchanges of words but gateways to a realm where individual perspectives coalesce into a mosaic of understanding.

So embrace the discomfort, seek the unfamiliar, and engage in conversations that transcend the limitations imposed by societal constructs. In doing so, we reclaim our autonomy, nurture empathy, and inch closer to a world where conversations are not just about winning arguments but about fostering understanding, one dialogue at a time.

## Chapter Insights

- Many Americans have allowed their commitment to their own sense of being right, their own sense of political righteousness, to overshadow their commitment to what's closest to them.
- Civility isn't built overnight.

## Recommended Actions

- Don't leave an argument and say, "I'm done with this guy. I won't be back." Always return to the conversation because doing so preserves the ability to show respect and to learn from each other.
- Embrace the discomfort, seek the unfamiliar, and engage in conversations that transcend the limitations imposed by societal constructs.

---

### QUESTIONS FOR YOU

Civility isn't built overnight. It requires a commitment to keep returning to the conversation, to have the patience to see this value build over time. Are you ready for the journey that leads to civility? The questions that follow can help you explore how to get there.

Do you feel nervous, scared, worried, or any other emotion about the lack of civility in America? Could that be a contributing factor to impatience when it comes to civility-building?

Where do these feelings come from? What is the fear that lies beneath these emotions? Explore what you're afraid might happen if America slips into incivility and stays there.

With the idea that civility takes time to build, how might you prepare yourself for a longer journey to get there?

Going the distance often requires small wins along the way. How might you define a "win" in the effort to build civility?

# 8

# Civility in Community

Most people would rather live in a community than in isolation. Today, communities tend to be far more diverse than they were 50 years ago, when it was possible to spend your entire life in places where nearly everyone looked, believed, and behaved the same way you did.

That homogeneity is pretty much gone today. Now, living in a community demands an understanding of and respect for those who hold opposing beliefs or come from different places, cultures, and faiths.

"Social order involves individual claims to each other," said the late Dr. Robert Morrison MacIver, a Scottish sociologist and political scientist. "Communal life is characterized by reciprocal action, and the wonder of the universe is the essential harmony of personal values working in and through society."[1]

Most relationships depend on feelings of solidarity. People connect over shared beliefs or interests. Most Americans are likely to say similar things about why they appreciate living in the United States, with a variety of protected freedoms topping the list. And yet many Americans are wary of their fellow citizens who hold opposing political stances.

A Pew Research study on partisanship and political animosity in 2016 found that half of Republicans and Democrats are actually

---

[1] https://www.nature.com/articles/100124a0.

frightened of the other party.[2] As a result, we live in isolated silos, unwilling to reflect on why the other side believes as it does. This myopic perspective is reinforced by social media algorithms that make sure we see a steady stream of viewpoints we already hold and shield us from other perspectives.

There is benefit, however, in respectful disagreement. It can be healthy if it is used as a means of expanding our knowledge of an issue. "Often it is easy to agree on the goal, like better education and a stronger democracy, even if we disagree on how to get there," Joan Blades and John Gable wrote for AllSides.com.[3]

During our Civility Sessions, we stress the importance of not giving up on dialogue after hitting the first speed bump. "Almost no one changes their mind on any particular issue after one conversation, but if we learn anything, it's that we care about each other," write Blades and Gable. Relationships across divides are crucial for building a stronger democracy.

America has a proud tradition of individual freedom, personal rights, and the ability to carve your own path. It's an established ethos that everyone has a right to his or her own opinions without interference from the state or their fellow citizens. That's healthy for democracy, but it can make civil discourse challenging.

It helps to learn the value of understanding other perspectives and how they were formed. This requires a commitment to listening and a sincere attempt to analyze opposing arguments.

Talking across divides is the only way to live in a pluralistic society. Conversations are an essential part of how we learn about government and politics and are a key factor in the formation of political views.

Despite our national discord, Americans enjoy political jawboning—81 percent of people with consistently conservative

---

[2] www.pewresearch.org/politics/2016/06/22/partisanship-and-political-animosity-in-2016/.
[3] https://www.aspeninstitute.org/blog-posts/its-important-to-speak-to-people-you-dont-agree-with/.

political perspectives enjoy talking about politics, and 69 percent of those with liberal views feel the same, according to a Pew Research study. But not always when the discussion is with someone on "the other side."

A relatively new field of political psychology looks at how people come to their political beliefs. In 1960, only 4 percent of Democrats and 4 percent of Republicans said they'd be disappointed if their child married someone from the opposite political party, according to a study by the Inter-university Consortium for Political and Social Research. By 2018, that number had soared to 45 percent of Democrats and 35 percent of Republicans.[4]

What's more, scholars are looking at political partisanship in the context of social identity. How we vote is now aligned with a person's sense of self. Partisan identity offers a feeling of belonging just as religious affiliation might. And this partisan identity conditions people to be accepting of information that supports their beliefs and makes them skeptical of statements that don't.

Interestingly, when your political views are challenged, the brain regions that are stimulated are the same as where notions of personal identity, threat response, and emotion live.[5] Our politics have become a greater part of ourselves, which means more is at stake—or at least, we think this is the case.

But we need to cross these divides, and in a hurry, as we face overlapping and compounding crises at home and abroad. Instead of uniting us against common challenges, these existential events are further splitting us apart. Nowadays, we are choosing to live in isolated silos and growing increasingly wary of stepping outside of our comfortable bubbles to encounter or engage with someone very different from us.

---

4 www.icpsr.umich.edu/web/ICPSR/studies/7201/versions/V2.
5 www.cnn.com/2017/01/03/health/political-beliefs-brain/index.html.

Even our homes offer no respite. More than half of Americans report divisions in their own families over politics.[6] We must find ways to talk things through. This is an urgent need, which apparently many Americans recognize, considering that there are nearly 8,000 "bridge-building" organizations in America today, including the Great Lakes Civility Project, for just this purpose. These bipartisan efforts are trying to stimulate dialogue and build civility so that we can move forward from a place of understanding and trust. There is even a bipartisan Select Committee for the Modernization of Congress that is "trying to dismantle the culture of disdain, dysfunction and division."[7]

Unless we decide we'd rather live alone than as part of a community, we must strive to understand one another. The only way to get there is by willingly engaging in civil conversation with people who hold different beliefs. America has long been a home for a variety of peoples from a variety of places, traditions, and belief systems. Many Americans once believed that was what made our nation special.

## Chapter Insights

- "Communal life is characterized by reciprocal action, and the wonder of the universe is the essential harmony of personal values working in and through society."
- A Pew Research study on partisanship and political animosity in 2016 found that 50 percent of Republicans and Democrats are actually frightened of the other party. As a result, we live in silos, unable to reflect on why the other side believes as it does.
- Despite our discord, Americans enjoy political jawboning—81 percent of people with consistently conservative political perspectives

---

6 time.com/6270884/americans-tackle-political-division-together/.
7 time.com/6270884/americans-tackle-political-division-together/.

enjoy talking about politics, and 69 percent of those with liberal views feel the same, according to Pew Research.

## Recommended Actions

- There are nearly 8,000 "bridge-building" organizations in America trying to stimulate dialogue and build civility so that we can move forward to a place of understanding and trust. The appendix of this book includes a list of civic and civility organizations you can get involved with.

> ### QUESTIONS FOR YOU
>
> When was the last time you engaged with someone who held different beliefs from you? What was that experience like?
>
> How might you benefit from a conversation with someone who holds opposing political beliefs? What emotions arise when you consider doing so?
>
> If you've been hesitant to encounter individuals who think differently from you, what might motivate that hesitation? And how might your world open up by stepping outside your comfort zone?
>
> If you don't know anyone who votes, practices, or believes differently, how might you engage with people who do? As a curiosity experiment more than anything!

# 9

# Acting Where You Have Agency

Every time we talk with groups or individuals about the Civility Project, this is the question that pops up at the end: *Where do we begin?*

People are really receptive to the concept of a better, more civil way to have conversations or disagreements. They enjoy the story about us, how deeply we disagree, and how we have found our way to a space where we can have difficult debates or arguments without being uncivil. And they grasp the pillars—the rules, if you will—that we have come to use in our discourse. In theory, it all works. It all makes sense and seems to point to a better way.

But there are so many things about our current discourse and culture that suggest incivility is an overwhelming problem with an out-of-reach solution. So much of what we see or hear or experience about our political and other disagreements says to us there's nothing we, as individuals, can do about it. Frustration is the feeling we are left with, more than anything else. We don't think that's by accident.

Part of the "sell" of modern media in particular is a kind of foreboding—a sense that what's happening in the world is so big and so complex that it's out of reach for the average person. There's nothing you can do. It's all way out of control.

That constant sense of urgency and trepidation brings viewers and listeners and readers back, over and over. Anxiety is a hell of a drug when it's sprinkled over information.

Think about cable news and its 24-hour cycle. Turn it on at any point during the day, and you're guaranteed to be greeted by language that's a bit overheated and framing that suggests eternal conflict about nearly everything. This is why the little banner across the bottom of the screen (we call them "lower thirds" in television lingo) reads "Breaking news." And it's why the assembled panels that debate the news during the day feature bombast and aggression, often over reason or actual give-and-take debate.

The medium is designed to keep you watching by suggesting that your role in all this is simply to be anxious, to believe that whatever the issue, the sky is falling.

Social media may be worse.

The norms and customs that guide so many of our online interactions are designed to inspire doubt—in each other, in the well-being of our culture and nation, in the very idea that things are OK. That we will be OK. Social media encourages the creation of self-censored social circles, places where we can freeze out anyone who doesn't conform to the prevailing sensibilities. And the tools of social media all inspire political and cultural isolation. We can block. We can mute. We can "unfriend" someone. All in an effort to curate the ideas around us, to push away what we don't agree with or understand.

As we wrote earlier in the book, it's not enough just to shut people out. It has become a habit to announce to everyone else that we've blocked or unfriended someone so the folks within our social circle can cheer us on, bolstering our own views in the process.

It all reinforces a sense that we are only in control of the familiar, of what we know. And we are helpless—or foolish—to even pursue the idea that we might expand our circle or find a way to manage the discomfort so it doesn't feel so debilitating.

The height of this sense of helplessness and frustration materialized during the January 6, 2020, insurrection at the US Capitol. Whether you voted for or supported Donald Trump or Joe Biden, most Americans didn't know, couldn't relate to, and on some level, just didn't understand how a group of fellow Americans had become so frustrated and unhappy that they were willing to violently disrupt the constitutional transfer of power in our nation.

As glass broke, objects got hurled, and Capitol police officers were battered, it was nearly impossible to discern how America had reached such a low point or how most Americans could see clear of the chaos and violence to even connect with the perpetrators—let alone try to understand them or their motivations.

But rather than give up, which many Americans seem to be doing, what we counsel is a reframing of actions and expectations. None of us, as individuals, has the opportunity to move the needle on civil discourse in a global sense. The nation is too large and too splintered, and the tools for persuasion or even dialogue are too blunted by the disparate and sometimes vicious nature of our disagreements.

Instead, what each of us *can* do is change the dynamic within our own lives, with the people we interact with every day. We call it acting where you have agency, and it's a great first step toward creating more civil space in our lives.

Think of the places we go and the people we see. Our neighbors. People in our school or religious communities. People in our families.[1]

That last group is critically important right now. The shape of our political discourse has become so distorted that it threatens the most fundamental relationships we have.[2] There are still far too

---

[1] www.npr.org/2020/10/27/928209548/dude-i-m-done-when-politics-tears-families-and-friendships-apart.

[2] www.foxnews.com/media/young-americans-skipping-family-gatherings-avoid-political-disagreements-survey.

many people now avoiding family interactions because of political differences.

Think about how damaging and hurtful that is. Politics and ideology are important parts of who we are, but how could they ever supplant familial bonds? How could our politics become so important that we would turn our backs on people who've been with us our whole lives, who shaped our lives in ways that no one else could or should?

Our families—like others close to us—are more easily reached to repair broken relationships or create opportunities for useful, noninjurious discourse. Using the pillars that we have outlined in this book already, your best chance to build strong relationships that feature civil dialogue about difficult subjects is with the people closest to you.

Stephen learned this in a difficult way with an aunt and uncle who are deeply Republican and committed to arguing in favor of conservative politics and approaches at nearly every turn. (His aunt recently passed away.)

For years, they watched a lot of Fox News and listened to a lot of conservative talk radio and then would spend long hours writing emails or text messages to family about the things they saw and learned. (Nolan jokes that he pays for their subscriptions.) Over time, Stephen developed a dread of receiving his relatives' emails or texts. It was like visiting the old-school mailbox and anticipating bad news from the IRS or receiving hate mail from a neighbor.

The rest of the family was not too interested in fighting over these ideas, either. The conservative aunt and uncle became more the subject of other family members' discussions—Did you see what they sent last week? Do you ever answer them?—than the object of desired interactions. For a long time, Stephen just steered clear of engaging with them about their political beliefs. That meant accepting a distance that felt uncomfortable.

But a few years ago, Stephen began engaging more in the back-and-forth with his conservative relatives. He began dropping the assumptions that there was something "wrong" with the way they were thinking or that their beliefs didn't deserve respect.

He set reasonable expectations for interactions with them—not to humiliate or denigrate or even convince but to listen and learn and understand. And he committed to elevating the value of the relationship with them above all things political.

Stephen's aunt and uncle visited Detroit in November of 2018 for Thanksgiving—just two years after Donald Trump was elected president. There was a lot of heated anticipation about their presence. Some of Stephen's family members were worried that their exuberance for the still-new president would land like a boulder in the middle of the Thanksgiving table, inspire fights, and maybe ruin the holiday.

But Stephen made a point about the charm and accessibility of the moment: this was family, not strangers, coming to dinner. There were a million things to discuss and think about together before even veering into politics. And the most important truth was that the visiting aunt and uncle hadn't been to Detroit in nearly a decade.

Stephen led a prayer before dinner that emphasized the power of family connection and the lure of renewed fellowship with loved ones. He ribbed his aunt and uncle a bit about "crossing over into enemy territory," but it was well received and didn't spark any trouble.

Dinner conversation didn't avoid politics but didn't center on it, either. Despite the tense times, family was the focus of everyone's interactions, and most political talk was expressed in terms of worry—a feeling common to everyone present regardless of their support of or disdain for Trump.

A few nights later, the family gathered again in the private dining room at the Saint Regis Hotel in Detroit's New Center neighborhood to celebrate Stephen's birthday. Stephen took the liberty that came with the attention on him to start a conversation about the country's deep divides and the way it had split families.

The reaction, at first, was tense. But with coaxing, everyone wound up actually discussing the issues—not just civilly but in an engaging and even cooperative fashion.

There wasn't agreement, and no one backed away from what they believed. But the constructive tone of the disagreements was refreshing—both for what it represented in the moment and for what it meant in a bigger sense.

Everyone there was acting in a space where they had agency, where they had credibility and the ability to shape the interactions intentionally and with good intent. That's a key part of the potential for success as well. When we act in our most close-in spaces—family, neighborhood community, school or religious community—we are more likely to feel like we are all on an even footing. That balance fuels the agency that everyone has. It girds and protects it even as difficult or uncomfortable things might be said and heard.

At the birthday dinner with Stephen's aunt and uncle, no one felt as if their hand in things was disadvantaged or that they would be dismissed. People talked. People listened. And where deep disagreements came up, there wasn't an instant hostile reaction.

Of course, the success of that conversation did not fundamentally change the relationship anyone had with this conservative aunt and uncle. No one conversation could. But moving the interaction with them to a "safe" space of civility, of constructive dialogue where everyone had equal footing, made a difference going forward.

A lot of the aggressive emailing and texting stopped, and if politics came up during in-person interactions, the tone was much more reasonable, on all sides, and less likely to result in sharp exchanges or, just as bad, avoidance.

In the years since, Stephen has been working consistently to build on what started at that Thanksgiving gathering. Striving for civility where you have agency is a process, not an event. There is no end point—only the effort you can put in and the constant improvement you could realize as a result.

## Chapter Insights

- Politics and ideology are important parts of who we are, but how could they ever supplant familiar bonds?
- Our families—like others close to us—are more easily reached to repair broken relationships or create opportunities for useful, noninjurious discourse.

## Recommended Actions

- When looking to repair a family relationship, set reasonable expectations for interactions with them—not to humiliate or denigrate or even convince but to listen and understand.
- Remember to find the common ground with your family—your history, favorite stories, catching up on how people are doing with work, school, with a health issue, and so on. There are a million things to discuss and think about together before even veering into politics.

### QUESTIONS FOR YOU

Now that you've considered a lot of the factors and research offered in this book about why incivility exists in America, reconsider some earlier questions (provided here) with new insights and see if your answers are different!

What are the most important issues that influence your political beliefs?

How did you come to your political beliefs? Are you comfortable with this? Why or why not?

Could anything convince you to vote for a different political party? Why or why not?

What are your honest opinions about people who vote differently from you?

What benefit might you gain from engaging in conversation with someone who votes differently than you?

# Conclusion
## Civility in Action

There's an ominous feeling about what's happening in America. We've been through polarizing times before and survived, but there's no guarantee we will this time.

Point in any direction to assign the blame: a rise in partisanship corresponding with the principle that all that matters in politics is gaining and holding power, social media and cable television outlets that profit from keeping us angry and frightened, and a growing conviction that those on the opposite bank are ignorant or evil. It all plays into this roiling sense that America is going to hell, and it's the other side's fault.

The threat to the foundation of our republic is what motivated us to take up the cause of civility. And in some ways, we're unlikely advocates. We certainly have spent our time in the public boxing ring. We are not mild mannered, nor are we shy about stepping on toes or throwing elbows, and we know we have hurt others' feelings. We're not always proud of our behavior, but we've learned from it.

That's why, in 2020, we founded the Great Lakes Civility Project, which seeks to bring people of opposing viewpoints together for meaningful discourse. In our programs, participants learn the pillars of civility and get a chance to engage in discussions as they learn to listen to others. This book takes it one step further, bringing the principles behind civility in interpersonal relationships to you with practical steps to introduce civility into your relationships.

"If we reach the point where we dehumanize the people we disagree with, anything is possible," Stephen says. "We must step back and learn to talk to people as people rather than political adversaries."

Our aim is to help individuals build personal relationships across the various divides, to measure people by something other than our differences. And to not contribute to the divisiveness.

We are not out to achieve consensus. Americans will never be in universal agreement on any issue, and it would be unhealthy for our democracy if they were. Dissent is a necessary element of a functioning republic. Vigorous debate on policy and politics provides a vital check on our governing system. Nations that demand a like-minded populace are, without exception, autocratic, repressive states.

What we're aiming for is to build respect between people who currently find no value in engaging with those who are different from them, whether the differences stem from politics, race, or culture. We are as different as two people can be in most of those areas. But we don't hate each other because of it. Rather, we've developed a strong mutual respect that comes from understanding the "why" behind our differences.

Our project is guided by the words of the Rev. Dr. Martin Luther King Jr., who in 1962 said in a speech at Iowa's Cornell College, "I am convinced that men hate each other because they fear each other. They fear each other because they don't know each other, and they don't know each other because they don't communicate with each other, and they don't communicate with each other because they are separated from each other."[1]

So let's start talking. Let's commit to understanding what shapes and motivates each other. And let's remember that, in the end, we all want the same things: peace, prosperity, and a better world for future generations. If we lose sight of what connects us

---

[1] https://news.cornellcollege.edu/dr-martin-luther-kings-visit-to-cornell-college/.

as Americans, we risk losing the freedoms and democratic ideals that all of us hold dear. Let's not waste any more time.

## Chapter Insights

- The Rev. Dr. Martin Luther King Jr. said, "I am convinced that men hate each other because they fear each other. They fear each other because they don't know each other, and they don't know each other because they don't communicate with each other, and they don't communicate with each other because they are separated from each other."

## Recommended Actions

- Start where you have agency (defined as the ability to act independently and have free choices based on one's will). This could be local or wherever you have relationships—for example, your immediate communities, family, neighborhood, school community, or religious community.
- Start small; take it one conversation, one relationship, one community at a time; and persist with a dedication to a purpose and a cause.
- Make sure you don't escalate a conversation; choose to deescalate instead.
- Remember that civility is not a quick process. But the more you treat people with respect, the more likely they are to learn from your example.

# Meet the People behind the Civility Project

## Nolan Finley

On the wall of my office hangs a photograph of the three-room house I was brought home to after my birth in the foothills of southern Kentucky. My mother was born in that house, and my father was born just a few miles away. I keep the picture on the wall to remind me where I come from, and not just as a place. I come as well from the region's customs, culture, religion, and politics. And although my parents brought us north in search of hope in Detroit's factories, they never let us forget where home was. That photo, more than anything else, reminds me of who I am and why.

Politically, I'm a conservative. I still say that even though what it means to be a conservative by popular definition has been twisted grotesquely since Ronald Reagan first gave it relevance for me.

As a young man, I was much affected by Jimmy Carter's malaise. Carter, bless his heart, was as fine a man as ever sat in the White House. But he was a lousy president.

I chafed at his admonishment that the good times for America were over and that as a people we had to accept less, live simpler, and take a smaller role in the world. That was tough to swallow for someone raised to believe hard work made anything possible. Carter's defeatism and my 12 percent first mortgage rate killed any possibility that I might drift into the Democratic Party.

President Reagan brought the Greatest Generation's "we can do anything" spirit to the White House, and corny as it sounds now, I bought into his vision of America as a shining city on the hill. Unfortunately, Reagan invited the religious right into the Republican Party, and that gave rise to the Tea Party, and ultimately, Donald Trump. Today's GOP is as unacceptable to me as the Democratic Party was back then. I'm often called a RINO—Republican in Name Only—for refusing to embrace this new version of the GOP.

That charge reminds me of the story of the farmer and his wife who drove to town every Saturday in their old pickup. On one trip, looking at the empty space on the bench seat between them, the wife said accusingly, "When we first married, we sat right next to each other in the truck."

The farmer looked at the seat, and then at her, and replied, "Well, I ain't moved none."

Neither have I. I'm still standing where I stood 45 years ago.

My conservatism is informed by a set of values that tip the balance of power sharply toward the individual and away from the government. I believe in the ability of the free marketplace to create broad wealth and opportunity. Conservative to me means advocating for small and efficient government and an economy unburdened by excessive regulation and taxation. For unfettered and mutually beneficial trade pacts. For a strong national defense and foreign alliances that serve America's interests. For immigration policies that meet the nation's need for talent, the immigrant's quest for opportunity, and the nation's requirement of secure borders. It's also for aid programs that encourage independence, not dependency. My stance supports the rule of law and respect for the Constitution as written.

True conservatives, in my mind, must be civil libertarians as well. I am extremely protective of the space the Constitution carves out for an individual to stand safe from the heavy hand of government. A free speech absolutist, my biggest worry today is the determination on both sides of our political divide to stifle speech and suppress the expression of contrary ideas. It's better to bring abhorrent beliefs to the surface where they can be debated and discredited than allow them to remain in the shadows, where they can fester into something dangerous.

While I believe principle should guide us, as a pragmatist, I also believe compromising does not mean selling out. There are times when practical governing demands bending principles to get a deal that allows us to move forward together.

On cultural issues, my conservative view is guided by the belief that everyone gets just one life, and each of us has the right to live it in a way that brings us happiness without government meddling. I'm also convinced you can't keep people from their vices no matter how many rules you write. Changing hearts is better than changing laws, and the legal code is a poor substitute for a fraying moral code. That's informed my opinions on everything from drug decriminalization to abortion.

Suspicion of the government is part of my genetic code. I joke that as a kid, if my family saw a government man coming down the road, we hurried to hide things, starting with Grandpa. My father refused to fill out my college federal aid form because, he said, "They're asking too many personal questions." I went to college anyway and was not only the first in my immediate family to do so but also the first to graduate from high school. Both of my parents left school after the eighth grade to go to work.

Work was expected in our family, and it was how we were valued. As a boy, I worked on my uncle's tobacco farm, hard work done almost entirely by hand. When I was with him, my uncle didn't have a tractor; he still farmed with a team of mules. As a high school junior, I got a job in a fiberglass parts plant on Detroit's west side, rushing from class to the factory for the afternoon shift. It was a pace I kept throughout my years as a student at Wayne State University.

I have little patience for those who refuse to work and believe public assistance should be reserved for those who can't. As long as there are vacant jobs in the economy, no able-bodied adult should get a check from the government.

One of the defining events of my childhood came when the union went on strike at the chemical plant where my father worked. We were already living on the financial edge, and even a short strike threatened our viability. Dad took on a series of temporary, backbreaking jobs to bring in money, the worst of which required him to lie in a pit welding railroad cars as they rolled above him. When I hear people say there are jobs Americans won't do, I think of the miserable jobs my father took to keep us afloat.

The union set up a center where families could get government commodities, and it killed my mother to take them. She hid the silver cans and cheese cartons deep in the pantry and cursed the union.

Years later, I found a letter she'd written to her sister asking to send presents so her three kids could have a Christmas. In the end, the nine-month strike was settled for a 10-cent-an-hour pay raise. Our family was nearly ruined for four bucks a week. I haven't had much use for unions since.

I'm also a Christian. We grew up serious Baptists who went to church twice on Sunday and to prayer meetings every Wednesday night. The church was the center of our social lives and nearly the sole source of our friends. My parents would do without rather than miss their 10 percent tithe obligation. That background, I hope, has given me a measure of compassion. And of fairness.

I've had people assume that my religious upbringing is the reason I'm such an ardent supporter of Israel. It's not. That stems from the massacre of Jewish athletes at the 1972 Olympics in Munich, where eight Palestinian terrorists killed two Israeli athletes and took nine more hostage simply because they were Jewish. Watching that unfold on television as a teenager seared in my mind the perilous position of Jews in a world that has never ceased trying to kill them. I'm proud to be the father of three children now grown to honorable adulthood and grandfather to five grandchildren on their way to such. I take no credit. The best thing I ever did for my kids was give them a good mother.

But I did try to raise them in the same culture in which I was brought up and with the same values. I believe a parent's job is to prepare their children to stand on their own, to let them make their own decisions and live with the consequences.

For my 12th birthday, I got a 20-gauge shotgun and hung it on my bedroom wall. Nothing seemed out of the ordinary about that. I saw guns in the homes of most of my friends and all of my relatives. Guns were not the terrifying things then that they are today.

I grew up hunting and still enjoy shooting sports. I know firsthand that most gun owners are safe and responsible. I also believe that without the Second Amendment, they would lose their guns to do-gooders who are convinced firearms are the root of a violent society rather than its tool. Coincidentally, guns are responsible for one of the most important relationships of my life.

I met John Dingell on Mackinac Island nearly 30 years ago during one of the Detroit Regional Chamber's policy conferences. For some reason, we started talking about hunting and guns and continued the conversation for three decades. His mission became to make me a better shotgunner, and we spent hours on the skeet range trying to make that happen. We also had some fine times in the duck blinds on Maryland's Eastern Shore, where John owned a few acres across the river from a hunting preserve. I was with John when he shot his last duck and when he fired a gun for the final time.

I was also with him when he was agonizing over the decision to retire after 59 years in the House of Representatives. And as he was drawing his last breaths. The most poignant moment of my life was watching the coroner carry John's flag-draped body out of his Dearborn home as the few of us there sang "America the Beautiful."

At first, it was hard for me to reconcile John's passion for guns with his otherwise liberal politics. The longest-serving congressman in American history was also one of its most progressive. John introduced a national health insurance bill in every session of Congress until Obamacare passed. Our politics could not have been more different.

And yet we could talk politics without getting stuck on the many points on which we disagreed. We just talked through them. John always listened before reacting, and I found that to be an important tool in maintaining a civil conversation. Listening to John talk about his battles, and his wins and losses, was like a master's-level course in political science.

I recall a day we were together when John was being bombarded with angry calls from environmentalists for supporting the interests of the auto companies and autoworkers in his district. He hung up, exasperated, and said, "They think they're the only ones who talk to God."

Most of us think that same thing, which is why it's so hard to accept that the person on the other side of the table is just as convinced of their righteousness as you are. My approach to opinion-making is to start with the possibility that I could be wrong and then get about finding out for certain.

I loved John Dingell as I've loved few people in my life. That relationship with John opened the door to the one with Steve. By the time I met Steve, it was no longer a novelty for me to find close friendship across the political divide. From John, who was truly civility personified, I had learned the value of opening myself to those who aren't exactly like me.

I've been a newspaperman my entire adult life, and almost entirely with *The Detroit News*. Perhaps the luckiest day of my life came on the night in 1976 when Don Pilette, my copyediting instructor at Wayne and an editor at the *News*, asked if anyone in the class was interested in a job as a copyboy.

Having just been laid off from the factory and uncertain how I'd pay my upcoming tuition bills, I quickly raised my hand. Looking around the classroom, I was relieved to see mine was the only one in the air. Except for a few months at the *Jackson Citizen Patriot* after my copyboy stint, I've spent most of the last half century at the *News*, a tenure split almost evenly between the newsroom and the editorial page. Looking back, I wouldn't change a thing.

## Stephen Henderson

I usually tell two stories to frame the way my life and experiences have shaped my sociopolitical outlook. One is about my father. The other is about my children.

My dad was born in Natchez, Mississippi, in 1933. This was the height of the Jim Crow era, which meant my dad attended schools that were segregated by law and had to fear he might become one of the 600 Black people murdered in the state during the lynching campaign of the early 20th century. He couldn't eat at lunch counters downtown or shop at stores. When he turned 18, he could register to vote—but racist tools like poll taxes or "literacy" tests meant he couldn't cast a ballot. Still, he grew up with enough patriotism and love for his country to volunteer to join the US Air Force and serve during the Korean War.

When he returned to Natchez as a war veteran, not much had changed in terms of his prospects. He still couldn't eat at downtown lunch counters or shop in many stores. He couldn't get many jobs because they didn't hire African Americans.

And he still could not vote. Yes, a man who put his life on the line to defend his country could not cast a ballot for the person who would lead that country. This, to me, has always been a cardinal American sin—that for every war up through Vietnam, Black veterans returned to a nation that still did not see them as whole or even human.

More importantly, in places like Mississippi, the GI Bill, framed to give war veterans a leg up on restarting their civilian lives, couldn't help Black men like my dad. His race prevented him from buying a house in the neighborhoods where government-backed mortgages were offered. Black people also couldn't gain admission to the schools where GI Bill tuition subsidies were available.

So the sting of the state-powered discrimination he faced in the Jim Crow South had intergenerational effects. The wealth-building that White veterans would begin with the strength of GI Bill benefits would pass Black veterans by. And again—this wasn't some distant relative I read about or heard stories about. This was my father—the first man I knew and the person whose life successes and failures would frame much of what would be possible in my own life.

This, unfortunately, is the legacy that nearly all African Americans my age were born into. It is a legacy of racism and curtailed opportunity, a legacy of struggle against that racism, and a hope that things could be better.

So much of American discourse today is hung up on trying to refute the current-day effects of this history. It's true that the strength of the civil rights movement produced the Civil Rights Act of 1964, the Voting Rights Act of 1965, and the Fair Housing Act of 1968. Legal segregation became illegal, and at least in name, America finally embraced equality.

But my father was in his mid-30s by the time any of that happened, and much of his life was already cast—especially his economic life. The truth is that before his death in the mid-1980s, he never managed to buy a home. He never got a college degree.

That meant everything to the circumstances into which I was born and the possibilities that welcomed me. Discrimination—legal discrimination that had its roots in 18th-century America—was the predicate for my life, which would stretch through the end of the 20th century and into the beginning of the 21st.

There is no way to see challenges and opportunities in America outside that context. The good news is that the trajectory of my life, which begins just after the civil rights movement's most poignant victories, confirms at least some of the promise of those hopes.

The American experiment does begin to grant fuller opportunity. Things do get better—not easily, but somewhat steadily. I get opportunities my father could only have dreamed about thanks to the victories of the civil rights movement and the momentum of racial progress that is embraced and harnessed by my parents' generation.

And by the time my children are born, in the first decade of the 21st century, their reality is shaped as much by racial progress, if not equality, as it is by the history of racial discrimination. It's exemplified in many ways, but perhaps best by their early learning about the nation in which they were born. The word *president*, for them, is first associated with Barack Obama, the nation's first African American president.

There are few countries in the world where that kind of progress is possible—moving, over two generations, from overt and systematic discrimination to a world where the victims of that discrimination can indeed succeed at the highest levels. Those bookends form the basis for the way I see politics and activism and culture today. America is a nation that was formed around a commitment to inequality, but its institutions also harbored the leverage points for the move to equality.

Sometimes people confront me and say, "Well, your whole outlook is about race. Why can't you get past that? Why do we need to keep talking about what happened before?"

I always answer simply: "Tell that to my father. America made race the issue in his life and in mine. We didn't. The call to us is to embrace the opportunity to make it matter less or not at all—not to pretend it doesn't matter."

What the path toward equality in this country has taught me, more than anything, is to have strong faith in the power of progressive institutions. America is about individual freedoms and rights—but for those who were initially locked out, progressive institutions were the way to actualize those freedoms and ensure they were respected.

Among the first of these institutions, of course, are this nation's foundational documents. While the Declaration of Independence and the Constitution are crippled early in the republic's formation by systemic racism, it's their aspirational nature that paves the way for progress. Phrases like "all men are created equal" and ideas like due process and antidiscrimination give tremendous power to the cause of justice and equality. The progress America has achieved has its feet firmly planted in those pillars.

Other progressive institutions leveraged those foundational ones to move the nation forward. The legacy of the civil rights movement—its reliance on Black churches and grassroots organizations—showed the power of collective action to secure and defend the individual rights that were promised, but originally denied, to so many Americans.

Unionism played a huge role too—even in my family. My mother's father, William Beckham Sr., was a key aide to Walter Reuther, the founder of the United Auto Workers. Reuther brought my father to Detroit from Cincinnati, where he had been working as a UAW organizer and negotiator, in the late 1950s to help the union align with Detroit's powerful civil rights organizations and growing Black political class.

The unions helped batter down the racist barriers to Black equality in the workplace and gave important strength to the cause of civil rights. They helped galvanize the tie between economic and social justice and ushered in the possibility of the Black middle class—free to work for fair wages and in fair conditions so it could also be free to pursue all the nation's other promises of equality.

The Jesuits also set an example of the power of progressive institutions and thinking. For 400 years, they've challenged the Catholic Church, and the rest of the world, to imagine a world in which social justice comes first—ahead of economic or selfish considerations. I studied with them for the 7th through 12th grades, at the University of Detroit Jesuit High School and Academy, and learned how to build a life around success that's focused on lifting up the principles of opportunity and fairness.

The sweep of progress over my life also has taught me a lot about the dangers of the alternative and the vigilance that's required to keep that progress growing. But it's still true that, on paper, this nation has only fully respected equality for around 60 of its nearly 250 years of existence—the 1965 passage of the Voting Rights Act completed the long journey toward legal disdain for the denial of equal rights.

The work isn't done, at least in terms of outcomes. African Americans still struggle with economic opportunity as well as with other inequalities. The instinct to "move beyond" the battle to overcome America's past is a desire to return to that past. It is, and always has been, the call of progressive institutions to push for something better and for the future. That shapes my outlook and my work—as a journalist, as a father, as a citizen—every day.

## Lynne Golodner

I wish I could say I'd had carefully thought-out political perspectives early in my life like Nolan and Stephen. I grew up rather privileged in a Detroit suburb, the eldest in a secular Jewish family and with a considerable amount of disposable wealth. To my own shame, I don't even think I realized how fortunate we were. We took yearly resort-style vacations, and my parents sent me and my two siblings to a month of sleepaway camp every summer starting from the age of nine.

My father, however, grew up in a modest family and first flew on an airplane when he was 18. To pay his way through Michigan State University, he had to wash dishes in a fraternity house and could never dream of becoming one of its members. Both of my parents grew up in Detroit. My father had a bar mitzvah but was otherwise not very observant in Judaism, yet he was taunted and assaulted for being Jewish. That led him to build strength by playing hockey, which he did until well into his 70s. He started his career as a teacher, then took an opportunity to begin working in the scrap metal industry, eventually becoming one of its leaders later in his career. In the first half of the 20th century, an estimated 80 to 90 percent of all scrap dealers were Jewish largely because Jews weren't welcomed into precious metals trading or traditional financial industries at the time.

My mother came from a more religious and more privileged family, with a father who was a first-generation American, born to Polish immigrants on New York's Lower East Side. On all sides of my family, I was two or three generations removed from immigrants from Eastern Europe and Russia who had fled pogroms. In my teens and 20s, I connected with the Jewish concept of *tikkun olam*, repairing the world, and became fiercely devoted to social justice, which led me to march in protests alongside African Americans and even apply to be the minority issues reporter at the *Michigan Daily*. I was mystified when I was told I couldn't because I wasn't a minority. As a Jew, I've always been aware of how different I am from the mainstream of America, though I can blend easily because of my light skin, and I've always been a minority, though without the empathy of other marginalized groups.

This led me to learn more about my Jewish roots, and I became Orthodox in my late 20s. I observed very strictly for a decade, during which time my liberal-leaning and feminist ideals were often at odds with conservative-voting friends who were guided only by which candidate would be a friend to the Jews and to Israel. My first visit to Israel was as a journalist in my mid-20s, and I felt like I'd come home. I left Orthodoxy at 37 and was relieved to return to my more progressive roots.

But it wasn't until I began working with the Civility Project that I took a hard look at why I believe the way I do—and discovered that I am not, in fact, as progressive as I thought. Because my people have not had an easy time being accepted into mainstream society, I believe in offering opportunities equally to all. And because my family had nothing but their own scrappiness to rely on when they came to America fleeing pogroms, I also believe that every person who reasonably can should work their hardest to make a better life for themselves. I straddle political narratives, occupying a centrist middle. As an entrepreneur and the daughter of an entrepreneur, I am conservative on financial matters, and because more people on the right support Israel than on the left, I lean right. Yet I lean left on many issues because my heart bleeds for people who do not have the same access to education and property or opportunities for progress that I was born into, and I believe those of us with privilege bear the responsibility of sharing it with those who don't. I believe people with more wealth should pay more in taxes than people with less. I am not convinced that capitalism is a good system, but I believe democracy is, and I won't vote for anyone I believe to be a danger to the future of our republic. That said, I think the biggest challenge facing our nation today is that capitalism and democracy really don't go together. One is survival of the economic fittest with the wealthy rising to the top, and the other is for the people, by the people—*all* the people.

Finally, I remain mystified about why Jews are the only marginalized population that is not welcomed as part of left-leaning movements advocating for equal rights and attention for all, and why Israel is the only nation in the world subjected to a continued double standard.

I have learned so much from working with Nolan and Stephen. Firm in their beliefs with the knowledge to back up their stances, they can approach a heated conversation with kindness and confidence. I'm not there yet, but I am paying close attention to them with every program we do and hope to one day be as adept as they are at this thing called civility.

# Acknowledgments

This book is an outgrowth of the work of the Great Lakes Civility Project, spearheaded by Nolan Finley and Stephen Henderson. The Civility Project would not exist without the generous support of Margaret Trimer at Delta Dental, Gary Torgow at Huntington Bank, and Dave Egner at the Ralph C. Wilson, Jr., Foundation. We owe a debt of gratitude to Sandy Baruah of the Detroit Regional Chamber for helping us get off the ground and for serving as our 501(c)3 for charitable donations.

We are grateful to all the organizations and corporations that have brought us to talk to their communities over the years. So many people are interested in and eager to participate in making America more civil, which gives us hope. Thank you to Professor Anthony Perry for partnering with us to create curriculum materials and for spearheading important civility programming at Henry Ford College. Thank you also to Dr. David A. Dulio, a distinguished professor of political science and director of the Center for Civic Engagement at Oakland University, for partnering with us in many ways over the years, including Civility Day programming on the campus of Oakland University, and for bringing us many civic partners in this effort. The Detroit Regional Chamber was the first organization to recognize the importance of this work and has been a supporter and partner of the Great Lakes Civility Project ever since.

# Appendix I
## A Civility Curriculum

The Great Lakes Civility Project has worked with universities and school districts, and we are pleased to share a curriculum created by Professor Anthony Perry at Henry Ford College that can be used in classes or small discussion groups to further civility-building. We are honored to partner with Henry Ford College and thank them for allowing us to include this in our book.

## Issue-Building Discussion and the Need-Demand-Response Model

The following discussion activity is a way for classes or groups to focus on common concerns and develop an appreciation for different perspectives, learn how to work collaboratively, and begin to understand the relationship between citizenship and participatory democracy.

The need-demand-response model focuses on how ordinary citizens can play a more direct role in the setting of the political agenda, or the list of concerns that government and leaders are trying to solve. The needs in this model are the issues or concerns. Demands are the mechanisms used to articulate the importance of concerns. The responses are the actions taken by the government, groups, or others to try to address an issue.

This activity has been used in a variety of settings including college introductory American government courses, in K–12 schools, and among conference attendees at peace and conflict conferences and seminars.

The activity begins with establishing a way to empower participants constructively by having them brainstorm what they consider to be the most pressing societal concerns at various levels. Depending on the event or level of individual training, this model can be used minimally as an icebreaker or to develop effective strategies for empowering participants with the skills of coalition-building and issue advocacy within a democratic society.

# Phase 1: Developing an Issues Agenda

### STEP 1

Break participants into small groups of three to five individuals to begin a dialogue about the most pressing concerns.

(Time: 20–30 minutes.)

Have participants discuss the following question:

**What are the most pressing issues/concerns facing (a) your community, (b) the United States, (c) the world?**
*[Community is defined by the participants. The issue should be concerns that require a societal response. The response could come from government, community organizations, nonprofits, private corporations, or a combination of these. Yet the issue is something that requires more than a response from an individual or a small group of individuals.]*

While the list of issues can be long immediately following the initial brainstorming, the goal is to have each individual focus on one to two of the issues that they think should be the priority. See if there is any consensus for what (a), (b), and (c) may be. Groups should be instructed to focus on the issues/concern, not any solution or particular causes, during this phase of the process.

It is important to have participants only focus on the concern. Many times an issue is widely accepted as a problem or a concern by individuals from across the political spectrum. Communication breakdown and disagreement begin with *how* to address the concern. For instance, healthcare costs, gun violence, and drug abuse are often universally seen as problems in American politics. Yet solutions often divide people on ideological and partisan lines. We must develop a common understanding that we agree that a problem must be addressed before we begin arguing about solutions.

Moreover, solutions to problems are controlled not by ordinary Americans but by those who can implement policy. Citizens often get dragged into partisan politics, having a consensus on the problem but then arguing over the details of policy that they are often not in a position to implement. This intensifies partisan discourse and prevents developing trust in leaders. It also contributes to treating politics as a team sport where we support our team and our team's leaders no matter the stance. This undermines citizens' role in democracy.

If people understand their role as citizens of a democracy first, then they are an essential check on tyranny. When citizens don't understand this role and believe that supporting the stance of those they believe are their leaders is primary, then they become tools of the party or ideological group. In such cases, civil discourse is easily undermined. Citizens are often easily manipulated into believing the other side is not only wrong but evil.

## STEP 2

Have small groups report what issues they deem to be priorities at each level (community, US, world). If you are doing this as a single-day activity, then have the small groups narrow their lists by consensus. That is, if a participant insists that a given issue be listed, then it will be included; however, see if the groups can narrow their lists to just the top priorities.

(Time: The amount of time you allow for Step 2 will depend on the size of the group. For overall attendance larger than 30, this can be done through written communications or a combination of small group discussions with reports back to the larger group.)

*[One effective way to focus the discussion after Step 2 is to end the report-out phase by asking all participants to consider what they believe is the most pressing concern and instructing them to be ready to shout their answer. Tell participants that in a democracy, citizens have a political voice to articulate their concerns. If we want elected officials to represent us, then we must ensure they hear our voices.*

*Give the participants a countdown and ask them, all at once, to express their concern as loudly as possible. If it is not loud, repeat to get participants to shout out their concern. This is an engaging activity that helps build buy-in to the process.*

*Generally, a lot of noise comes from the participants as they try to make sure "their" concern is heard by everyone. Which, of course, is difficult to actually achieve!*

*Ask the participants, "What was that?" Some will answer with their issue, others will say they don't know. Explain that they were asked to use their political voice to express their concerns and all you heard was noise!*

*One way to develop a political voice is to speak in unison. There are many societal concerns, and often it seems like none of these concerns are being addressed. One way to focus is to narrow the list of concerns. Ask participants to see if they can narrow their lists down to what they think needs to be the top concern(s) addressed now.*

*Then let participants know that just because "their" issue is not a top concern immediately, it does not mean it's not important or won't get attention later on. Sometimes focusing on "low-hanging fruit"—the issues that most participants are on board with—can help create a clear demand.]*

If the activity is a multiple-day activity, such as with a semester-long class, you can have participants seek out others beyond their classmates to expand the viewpoint. For instance, ask students to talk to family, friends, and neighbors about what they view as the most pressing concerns and why. You can also ask the participants to go out and find information that supports why the concern should be a priority. That is, what do the data or other compelling stories illustrate about the concern?

The exercise may include some concerns that are not widely seen as top priorities for all participants, but it is still important to allow participants' voices to be heard. The process is inclusive, and many times the minority concern, if well articulated, can become more mainstream.

Also, there may be issues on which participants are diametrically opposed to each other like pro-life/pro-choice positions on abortion. However, the goal is first to see what societal issues are seen as important by participants and why participants believe a certain concern deserves greater attention and focus from society and from community, political, and corporate leaders.

## STEP 3

Narrow the list of issues and develop an issues agenda.

(Time: Minimum of 5 minutes but can take up to an hour.)

The agenda should, at most, be 7 to 10 issues, depending on group size. For groups of less than 50, a narrower agenda of 3 to 4 issues is ideal.

Participants vote on what they deem to be top concerns. The vote can be done in a variety of ways. Time and group size often dictate how the voting process will go.

The key to the vote is not the outcome; it is to make sure participants feel that

1. the final agenda (the list of issues developed) was developed in a fair, open, and inclusive way;

2. they can support the agenda in principle, even if their top concern was not on the agenda; and

3. they understand that if they work collaboratively to articulate an issue of concern, they will have a better chance of using their political voice in an effective way.

## Voting Methods

- Allow participants to have multiple votes and weigh them toward one or more issue
- Ranked-choice voting
- Single-issue voting

Group size and the time you have for the voting process will determine which methods you employ, including the use of electronic voting or paper ballot or even an open caucus-type voting where participants stand with their issue group.

# Phase 2: Issue Advocacy

If this activity is being done over the course of several weeks or a semester, then it is easy to incorporate issue advocacy activities.

*[Issue advocacy focuses on the **concern**, not solutions. Competing solutions can be discussed and advocated as options as long as participants are reminded that the goal is to **solve the problem**—and that any given solution is secondary. If a solution is adopted but doesn't solve the issue, then trying other solutions should become part of the process until the issue is resolved.]*

Participants can engage in both direct advocacy and interest advocacy. The focus in this phase is to teach participants how to build and keep a coalition of people together, even if they may not agree on a particular solution but share a belief that an issue needs resolution.

Advocacy around lobbying has occurred where participants are lobbying not for any given solution but to share their concerns with elected officials as well as potential directions that these officials should consider when setting legislative priorities.

# Appendix II
## Civility Resources

We are thrilled to be among some incredible initiatives to build civility across America. This section is full of resources to further the civility conversation!

*The Soul of Civility: Timeless Principles to Heal Society and Ourselves* by Alexandra Hudson (St. Martin's Press, 2023)

Description: Alexandra Hudson, daughter of the "Manners Lady," was raised to respect others. But as she grew up, Hudson discovered a difference between politeness—a superficial appearance of good manners—and true civility. In this book, Hudson sheds light on how civility can help bridge our political divide. From classical philosophers like Epictetus, to great 20th-century thinkers like Martin Luther King Jr., to her own experience working in the federal government during one of the most politically fraught eras in our nation's history, Hudson examines how civility—a respect for the personhood and dignity of others—transcends political disagreements. Respecting someone means valuing them enough to tell them when you think they are wrong.

*Choosing Civility: The Twenty-Five Rules of Considerate Conduct* by P. M. Forni (St. Martin's Griffin, 1999)

Description: Most people would agree that thoughtful behavior and common decency are in short supply, or simply forgotten, in hurried lives of emails, cell phones, and multitasking. In *Choosing Civility*, P. M. Forni identifies the 25 rules that are most essential in connecting effectively and happily with others. *Choosing Civility* is a simple, practical, measured handbook on the lost art of civility and compassion.

*Mastering Civility: A Manifesto for the Workplace* by Christine Porath (Balance, 2016)

Description: Incivility is silently chipping away at people, organizations, and the economy. Slights, insensitivities, and rude behaviors cut deeply, and incivility hijacks focus. Even if people want to perform well, they can't. Customers too are less likely to buy from a company with an employee who is perceived as rude. Ultimately, incivility cuts the bottom line. In *Mastering Civility*, Christine Porath shows how people can enhance their influence and effectiveness with civility. Combining scientific research with evidence from popular culture and fields such as neuroscience, medicine, and psychology, this book provides managers and employers with a much-needed wake-up call while also reminding them what they can do to improve the quality of their workplaces.

*I'm Just Saying: A Guide to Maintaining Civil Discourse in an Increasingly Divided World* by Milan Kordestani (Simon & Schuster, 2023)

Description: A straightforward look at the history and art of maintaining courteous communication in an increasingly divided world. Milan Kordestani shows that although challenging conversations can be unpleasant, they can also help us grow. Kordestani uses contemporary case studies and personal experience to teach readers how to have constructive conversations by engaging in civil discourse—the idea that good-faith actors can reach a consensus on any opinion-based disagreement. He addresses the challenges that digital media consumption presents when seeking common ground, especially when people are only digitally connected.

*Civility: Manners, Morals and the Etiquette of Democracy* by Stephen L. Carter (Basic Books, 1998)

Description: Yale law professor Stephen Carter meditates on the "prepolitical" qualities on which a healthy society is based. Why do people show poorer manners today than in previous ages? How did we come to confuse rudeness with self-expression and acting on our "rights"? Carter looks at these and other important questions. There are messages here about generosity and trust, about respecting diversity and dissent, and about resolving conflict through dialogue rather than mandate.

*Rules of Civility & Decent Behaviour in Company and Conversation* by George Washington (Applewood Books, 1989)

Description: Copied out by hand as a young man aspiring to the status of gentleman, George Washington's 110 rules were based on a set of rules composed by French Jesuits in 1595. The first English edition of these rules was available in Francis Hawkins's *Youths Behavior, or Decency in Conversation amongst Men*, which appeared in 1640, and it is from this work that Washington seems to have copied. The rules as Washington wrote them out are a simplified version of this text. However much he may have simplified them, these precepts had a strong influence on Washington, who aimed to always live by them. The rules focus on self-respect and respect for others through details of etiquette. The rules offer pointers on such issues as how to dress, walk, eat in public, and address one's superiors.

*Differ We Must: How Lincoln Succeeded in a Divided America* by Steve Inskeep (Penguin Press, 2023)

Description: NPR host Steve Inskeep illuminates President Abraham Lincoln's life through 16 encounters with people who differed from him. While Lincoln didn't always change his critics' beliefs—many went to war against him—he learned how to make his beliefs actionable. He knew his limitations and, as history came to prove, knew how to prioritize. Many of Lincoln's greatest acts came about through engagement with people he disagreed with—and these disagreements made him the leader we still revere today.

*The Character of Nations: How Politics Makes and Breaks Prosperity, Family, and Civility* by Angelo Codevilla (Hachette Book Group, 2009)

Description: In the aftermath of the Cold War, people reexamined and reinvented political systems, conscious that political choices implied different ways of life. In this cross-cultural study, Angelo M. Codevilla shows that as people shape their governments, they shape themselves. Drawing broadly from history, from the Roman Republic to Alexis de Tocqueville's America, as well as from personal and scholarly observations of the 20th century, *The Character of Nations* reveals remarkable truths about the effects of government on a society's economy, moral order, family life, and ability to defend itself. Codevilla argues that in present-day America, government has had a profound negative effect on societal norms. It has taught people to seek prosperity through connections with political power, it has fostered the atrophy of civic responsibility, it has waged a war against family and religion, and it has dug a dangerous divide between those who serve in the military and those who send troops to risk their lives. Informative and provocative, *The Character of Nations* shows how the political decisions we make have higher stakes than simply who wins elections.

*Bonds of Civility: Aesthetic Networks and the Political Origins of Japanese Culture* by Eiko Ikegami (Cambridge University Press, 2005)

Description: Eiko Ikegami presents a complex history of social life in which aesthetic images became central to Japan's cultural identities. The people of premodern Japan built on earlier aesthetic traditions in part for their own sake but also to find space for self-expression in the increasingly rigid and tightly controlled Tokugawa political system. In so doing, they incorporated the world of the beautiful within their social life, which led to new modes of civility. They explored ways of associating while immersing themselves in aesthetic group activities.

*Rudeness and Civility: Manners in Nineteenth-Century Urban America* by John F. Kasson (Macmillan Publishers, 1991)

Description: This book explores the history and politics of etiquette from America's colonial times through the 19th century. The author describes the transformation of our notion of "gentility" and the development of etiquette as a middle-class response to the new urban and industrial economy and the excesses of democratic society.

*The Case for Civility: And Why Our Future Depends on It* by Os Guinness (HarperOne, 2008)

Description: "How do we live with our deepest differences, especially when those differences are religious and ideological?" The place to begin to search for answers is the United States. Not because the problem is worse here than elsewhere but because America has the best resources and therefore the greatest responsibility to point the way in answering deep questions. Guinness makes a passionate plea to put an end to the culture wars that threaten to reverse the principles our founders set into motion that have long preserved liberty, diversity, and unity in this country. Rich with historical anecdotes that unlock the genius of the American experiment, Guinness also takes on the contemporary threat of both the religious right and the secular left to construct a new way forward in the midst of the buildup to the fall 2008 presidential elections.

*Politics for People: Finding a Responsible Public Voice* by David Mathews (University of Illinois Press, 1999)

Description: David Mathews points out that many Americans, making no secret of their anger at being shut out of the political system, are looking for ways to take that system back. Because of their low opinion of "politics as usual," some people are trying to create a politics relevant to their everyday lives. In *Politics for People*, Mathews describes how people become politically engaged, how they build civic communities, and how they generate political energy. He explains what a democratic citizenry must do if representative government is to perform effectively and shows how officials might work with, and not just for, the public.

*The Politics of Meaning: Restoring Hope and Possibility in an Age of Cynicism* by Michael Lerner (Addison-Wesley Publishing Company, 1997)

Description: Drawing on ideas presented in the Bible, Jewish teachings, and his experience as a psychotherapist, Lerner examines the roots of the discontent felt by so many Americans about our political system and explains how values can be put back into our broken politics.

*The Argument Culture: Stopping America's War of Words* by Deborah Tannen (The Ballantine Books, 1999)

Description: This book examines the way we communicate in public—in the media, in politics, in courtrooms, and in classrooms. In the argument culture, war metaphors pervade our talk and influence our thinking. We approach anything we need to accomplish as a fight between two opposing sides. The author shows how deeply entrenched this cultural tendency is and how it affects us every day, often causing damage.

*The Magic of Dialogue: Transforming Conflict into Cooperation* by Daniel Yankelovich (Simon & Schuster, 2001)

Description: Social scientist Daniel Yankelovich proposes that dialogue, when properly practiced, will align people with a shared vision and help them realize their full potential as individuals and as teams. Drawing on decades of research and using real-life examples, *The Magic of Dialogue* outlines specific strategies for a wide range of situations for managers, leaders, businesspeople, and other professionals to succeed in an economy where more players participate in decision-making than ever before.

*Chasing the Red, White, and Blue: A Journey in Tocqueville's Footsteps through Contemporary America* by David Cohen (Picador USA, 2003)

Description: Using *Democracy in America* as his model, British and South African journalist David Cohen retraces Alexis de Tocqueville's journey around America to observe how the balance between the rich and the poor has changed over the past 150 years. Traveling from New York to the Ohio River Valley, the Deep South, California, and finally to Washington, DC, Cohen captures an America where inequality is balanced by unquenchable hope.

*The Passion of the Western Mind: Understanding the Ideas That Have Shaped Our World View* by Richard Tarnas (Ballantine Books, 1993)

Description: Here are the great minds of Western civilization and their pivotal ideas, from Plato to Hegel, from Augustine to Nietzsche, from Copernicus to Freud. Richard Tarnas describes profound philosophical concepts simply but without simplifying them.

*Nonviolent Communication: A Language of Life* by Marshall B. Rosenberg (Puddle Dancer Press, 2015)

Description: Nonviolent communication is the integration of consciousness, language, communication, and influence. The purpose of nonviolent communication, presents the author, is to increase our ability to live with choice, meaning, and connection; to connect empathically toward building more satisfying relationships; and to share resources so everyone benefits.

*Bowling Alone: The Collapse and Revival of American Community* by Robert D. Putnam (Simon & Schuster, 2001)

Description: *Bowling Alone* surveys Americans' changing behavior over the decades, showing how we became increasingly disconnected from family, friends, neighbors, and social structures. Our shrinking access to the "social capital" that is the reward of communal activity and community sharing still poses a serious threat to civic and personal health, and these consequences have a new resonance for our divided country today. The author also addresses the pervasive influence of social media and the internet, which has introduced previously unthinkable opportunities for social connection—as well as unprecedented levels of alienation and isolation. This book shows how social bonds are the most powerful predictor of life satisfaction and how the loss of social capital is felt in critical ways, acting as a strong predictor of crime rates and other measures of neighborhood quality of life and affecting our health in other ways.

*An Ethic for Enemies: Forgiveness in Politics* by Donald W. Shriver Jr. (Oxford University Press, 1998)

Description: The 20th century witnessed violence on an unprecedented scale in wars that ripped into the fabric of national and international life. The question remains: How can nations—or ethnic groups, or races—after long, bitter struggles, learn to live side by side in peace? In *An Ethic for Enemies*, Donald W. Shriver Jr., president emeritus of Union Theological Seminary, argues that the solution lies in our capacity to forgive. Taking forgiveness out of its traditional exclusive association with religion and morality, Shriver says it has an important role in the secular political arena. The book examines three cases from recent American history—postwar dealings with

Germany and Japan and our continuing domestic problem with race relations—cases in which acts of forgiveness have had important political consequences. *An Ethic for Enemies* challenges us to confront the hatreds that cripple society and threaten to destroy us.

*Turning to One Another: Simple Conversations to Restore Hope to the Future* by Margaret Wheatley (Berret-Koehler Publishers Inc., 2009)

Description: "I believe we can change the world if we start talking to one another again." With this simple declaration, Margaret Wheatley proposes that people band together with colleagues and friends to create solutions for social change. Such change will come not from governments or corporations, she argues, but from thinking together in conversation.

*The Values Divide: American Politics and Culture in Transition* by John Kenneth White (Chatham House, 2002)

Description: This book explores the increasingly dominant role values play in public and private life, concluding that a serious rift in political and cultural values in America produced the astounding tie between George W. Bush and Al Gore in the 2000 presidential election. White argues that while politically important, this "values divide" goes much deeper than cultural conflicts between Republicans and Democrats. Citizens are reexamining their own intimate values—including how they work, live, and interact with each other—while the nation's population is rapidly changing. The answers to these value questions, White contends, have remade both American politics and popular culture.

*Faith and Politics: How the "Moral Values" Debate Divides America and How to Move Forward Together* by Senator John Danforth (Viking Penguin, 2006)

Description: As a former three-term Republican US senator from Missouri and an ordained Episcopal priest, John Danforth watched the changes in his party and the church with growing alarm. In this book, he shares his concerns and calls for change. Danforth speaks out against the religious right's conflation of its political agenda with a religious agenda. He argues that no one should presume to embody God's truth and castigates the religious right for its focus on wedge issues that drive people apart. He also provides a blueprint for moving forward based on years of political experience and a life of religious service.

*Reclaiming Civility in the Public Square: 10 Rules That Work* by Cassandra Dahnke (Wingspan Press, 2007)

Description: We have become a nation divided against ourselves with public discourse controlled by special interests blind to the needs of the larger community. There seem to be few places where true dialogue about issues affecting us as a nation is possible. Civility in the public square is a necessity for the preservation of American democracy. The opposite of civility is not simply incivility but the disintegration of civilized society. This book offers practical lessons on reincorporating civility in our interactions.

*This I Believe: The Personal Philosophies of Remarkable Men and Women*, foreword by Studs Terkel, edited by Jay Allison and Dan Gediman with John Gregory and Viki Merrick (Holt Paperbacks, 2007)

Description: Based on the NPR series of the same name, *This I Believe* features 80 Americans—from the famous to the unknown—completing the thought that the book's title begins. Each piece compels readers to rethink not only how they have arrived at their own personal beliefs but also the extent to which they share them with others.

*Common Ground: How to Stop the Partisan War That Is Destroying America* by Cal Thomas and Bob Beckel (HarperCollins, 2008)

Description: Inspired by their popular *USA Today* column, conservative Cal Thomas and liberal Bob Beckel unmask the hypocrisy of the issues, organizations, and individuals that created and deepened the partisan divide at the center of American politics. Thomas and Beckel explain how bipartisanship and consensus politics are not only good for the day-to-day democratic process but also essential for our nation's future well-being.

*The Third Side: Why We Fight and How We Can Stop* by William Ury (Viking Penguin, 2000)

Description: It takes two sides to fight but a third to stop. Distilling the lessons of two decades of experience in family struggles, labor strikes, and wars, William Ury presents a bold new strategy for stopping fights. He also describes 10 practical roles that people can inhabit every day to prevent destructive conflict. Fighting isn't an inevitable part of human nature, Ury explains, drawing on his work and training as an anthropologist. The third side can transform daily battles into creative conflict and cooperation at home, at work, and in the world.

*The Cure for Our Broken Political Process: How We Can Get Our Politicians to Resolve the Issues Tearing Our Country Apart* by Sol Erdman and Lawrence Susskind (Potomac Books, 2008)

Description: Record numbers of Americans fear that our political process is broken. Our nation faces unprecedented challenges, yet politicians spend most of their energy attacking one another, and no one offers a practical way to neutralize bitter partisanship. Sol Erdman and Lawrence Susskind have spent more than 30 years resolving political conflict. They show how and why our elections compel politicians to bicker endlessly. This book suggests ways to redesign elections so politicians win only if they produce useful results and negotiate practical solutions to pressing problems. And there is a step-by-step plan proving that ordinary citizens have the power to bring about big changes.

*Saving Civility: 52 Ways to Tame Rude, Crude & Attitude for a Polite Planet* by Sara Hacala (SkyLight Paths, 2011)

Description: Cyberbullying, hostile and polarizing political infighting, and tasteless and tactless behavior may be on the rise, but it doesn't have to be this way. Sara Hacala, a certified etiquette and protocol consultant, offers a definitive look at what civility means and how it can change the nature of everyday interaction. She goes beyond a superficial discussion of proper manners to present civility as a mindset that helps you embrace your connections to others and repair society. Tapping the wisdom of ancient spiritual luminaries as well as social science research, she provides 52 practical ways you can reverse the course of incivility.

*The Righteous Mind: Why Good People Are Divided by Politics and Religion* by Jonathan Haidt (Pantheon Books, 2013)

Description: Drawing on 25 years of research into moral psychology, Jonathan Haidt shows how moral judgments arise not from reason but from gut feelings. He shows why liberals, conservatives, and libertarians have such different intuitions about right and wrong, and he shows why each side is actually right about many of its central concerns.

*You're Not as Crazy as I Thought (but You're Still Wrong): Conversations between a Die-Hard Liberal and a Devoted Conservative* by Phil Neisser and Jacob Hess (Potomac Books, 2012)

Description: Americans have been divided along political lines for so long that they have forgotten how to talk to one another, much less how to listen. Many citizens who disagree politically still share a desire to work for the greater good. Phil Neisser, a self-described "left-wing atheist," first met Jacob Hess, a social conservative, at the 2008 proceedings of the National Coalition for Dialogue and Deliberation. After discovering a shared commitment to cross-party dialogue, they embarked on a yearlong attempt to practice what they preached. In this book they share the result by exploring the boundaries of core disagreements about morality, power, gender roles, sexuality, race, big government, big business, and big media.

*Civility and Democracy in America: A Reasonable Understanding* by Cornell Clayton and Richard Elgar (Washington State University Press, 2012)

Description: A true democracy sanctions the challenge of deeply held values and accepted societal standards, but in the United States today, some members of the political arena have abandoned respectful communication. Now, contentious political discourse stalls Congress more and more often. Personal attacks and character assassinations replace reasoned arguments and intelligent debate. Yet incivility has existed in various forms throughout American history, often preceding positive change. In March 2011, Washington State University hosted a conference to initiate a discussion about the role of civility in American democracy. Leading scholars focused on history, religion, philosophy, art and architecture, and media. *Civility and Democracy in America* includes 23 papers presented at that conference, offering insight from seasoned experts.

*Predisposed—Liberals, Conservatives, and the Biology of Political Differences* by John R. Hibbing, Kevin B. Smith, and John R. Alford (Routledge, 2013)

Description: Buried in many people and operating largely outside the realm of conscious thought are forces inclining us toward liberal or conservative political convictions. Our biology predisposes us to see and understand the world in different ways. These predispositions are responsible for a significant amount of the political and ideological conflict that marks human history. In this book, social scientists John Hibbing, Kevin Smith, and John Alford—pioneers in the field of biopolitics—present evidence that people differ politically not just because they grew up in different cultures or were presented with different information. The universal rift between conservatives and liberals endures because people have diverse psychological, physiological, and genetic traits. These biological differences influence much of what makes people who they are, including their orientations to politics.

*The Lost Art of Listening: How Learning to Listen Can Improve Relationships* by Michael P. Nichols (The Guilford Press, 2009)

Description: Author Michael P. Nichols explains what true listening is and why it's become a near rarity in modern life. He also teaches how to listen well and use these skills to improve relationships. Plus, readers learn about what listening isn't, why people don't listen, and obstacles to listening (especially defensiveness owing to emotional overreaction).

*How Civility Works* by Keith J. Bybee (Stanford University Press, 2016)

Description: Is civility dead? Americans ask this question every election season, but their concern is hardly limited to political campaigns. Doubts about civility regularly arise in just about every aspect of American public life. Rudeness runs rampant. News media are saturated with aggressive bluster and vitriol. Digital platforms teem with disrespect. In *How Civility Works*, Keith J. Bybee argues that the very features that make civility ineffective and undesirable also point to its power and appeal.

*Civility: A Cultural History* by Benet Davetian (University of Toronto Press, 2009)

Description: Many people believe there is a noticeable and marked decrease in mutual consideration in both public and private settings. Are we less civil now than in the past? Benet Davetian's book *Civility: A Cultural History* responds to this question through a historical, social, and psychological discussion of civility practices in England, France, and the United States.

*Treating People Well: The Extraordinary Power of Civility at Work and in Life* by Lea Berman and Jeremy Bernard, with a foreword by Laura Bush (Scribner, 2018)

Description: A guide to personal and professional empowerment through civility and social skills written by two White House social secretaries. Lea Berman, who worked for George and Laura Bush, and Jeremy Bernard, who worked for Michelle and Barack Obama, have written an entertaining and uniquely practical guide to personal and professional success in modern life. Their daily experiences at 1600 Pennsylvania Avenue taught them valuable lessons about how to work productively with people from different walks of life and with different points of view. The authors make a case for the importance of a return to treating people well in American political life, maintaining that democracy cannot be sustained without public civility.

*Let's Talk Politics: Restoring Civility through Exploratory Discussion* by Adolf G. Gundersen and Suzanne Goodney Lea (CreateSpace Independent Publishing, 2013)

Description: It has become fashionable to decry the decline of public discourse and civility. *Let's Talk Politics* explores why there is so much incivility plaguing our social discourse—from the town hall meeting to the extended family's holiday gathering. Rather than just describing the problem, this book outlines how any and all of us can be a part of the solution by creating more productive dialogues one conversation at a time.

*Dialogic Civility in a Cynical Age: Community, Hope, and Interpersonal Relationships* by Ronald C. Arnett and Pat Arneson (Southern Illinois University Press, 1999)

Description: *Dialogic Civility in a Cynical Age* offers a philosophical and pragmatic response to unreflective cynicism. Considering that each of us has faced inappropriate cynical communication in families, educational institutions, and the workplace, this book offers insight and practical guidance for people interested in improving their interpersonal relationships in an age of rampant cynicism.

## Organizations and Media Outlets

**The Institute for Civility**—www.instituteforcivility.org

Since 1997, the Institute for Civility has been working to promote civility in government, workplaces, schools, and anywhere people gather to live, learn, work, and play. In 2023, the organization updated its name from the Institute for Civility in Government to better reflect the broad scope of our reach. It is a grassroots, nonpartisan, nonprofit organization that is building civility in a society that all too often seems tilted toward uncivil speech and actions. The institute does not endorse any political candidate, nor take a position on any issue. It's focused on process, not position.

**The National Institute for Civil Discourse at the University of Arizona**—nicd.arizona.edu

In 2011, the University of Arizona created NICD after the Tucson shooting that killed 6 people and wounded 13 others, including former congresswoman Gabrielle Giffords. Before the shooting, Congresswoman Giffords was already in discussion with the university about creating a center to study how to improve the quality of civil conversation. NICD is devoted to the principles that motivated Congresswoman Giffords—above all, holding the belief that people with different values and political preferences can discuss their differences in a civil and productive manner. The galvanizing power of that event brought together an impressive bipartisan group of leaders to work on these issues.

**Two Paths America**—www.twopathsamerica.com/civility

A dozen of America's most prominent thought leaders have been named as members of a new National Advisory Committee for Two Paths America, helping promote center-right solutions to some of the major issues facing our nation. Two Paths America is an organization created to promote reasonable and proven solutions to America's challenges. Members include Tom Davis, former member of the US House of Representatives (Virginia); Charlie Dent, former member of the US House of Representatives (Pennsylvania); Mickey Edwards, former member of the US House of Representatives (Oklahoma); Jennifer Horn, former chair of the New Hampshire Republican Party; Bob Inglis, former member of the US House of Representatives (South Carolina); John Kasich, former governor of Ohio; Bill Kristol, former editor-at-large of the *Weekly Standard*; Steve Luczo, chairman of Seagate Technology; Chad Mayes, a former member of the California State Assembly; Tom Rath, former attorney general of New Hampshire; Arnold Schwarzenegger, former governor of California; Rick Snyder, former governor of Michigan; and Christine Todd Whitman, former governor of New Jersey. The organization has five focus areas, including returning civility to public discourse, fixing the political party system, promoting bipartisanship, increasing voter participation, and addressing government accountability and ethical conduct in government.

**Listen First Project**—www.listenfirstproject.org/listen-first-blog/2018/10/31/rather-than-argue-over-civility-lets-listen-first-to-understand

The Listen First Project aims to help bridge divides in America. The organization connects the efforts of 500 Listen First Coalition partners, bringing people together. It manages national campaigns and strategies for social cohesion.

**The Deliberative Democracy Lab at Stanford University**—deliberation.stanford.edu

The Deliberative Democracy Lab (formerly the Center for Deliberative Democracy), housed within the Center on Democracy, Development and the Rule of Law at Stanford University, is devoted to research about democracy and public opinion obtained through Deliberative Polling.

**The Better Arguments Project**—betterarguments.org

The Better Arguments Project is a national civic initiative created to bridge divides and help people have better arguments.

**Facing History & Ourselves**—www.facinghistory.org

Facing History & Ourselves uses lessons of history to challenge teachers and students to stand up to bigotry and hate.

**Braver Angels**—braverangels.org

Braver Angels is the nation's largest cross-partisan, volunteer-led movement to improve American politics. Through community gatherings, debates, and grassroots leaders working together, it's trying to help America overcome the bitterness of pervasive partisan divide.

**Living Room Conversations**—livingroomconversations.org

Living Room Conversations connects people across divides including politics, age, gender, race, nationality, and more through guided conversations proven to build understanding and transform communities.

**Make America Dinner Again**—www.makeamericadinneragain.com

Since 2016, this organization has convened nationwide small-group conversations to bridge divides. People are invited to sit down to dinner together for respectful conversation, guided activities, and delicious food.

**More in Common**—www.moreincommon.com

Driven by a mission to understand the forces driving people apart, find common ground, and bring people together to tackle shared challenges, More in Common has teams in the United States, the United Kingdom, Poland, Germany, and France. Specific strategies differ according to where they believe they can make the most positive impact. International teams share a vision of building more united and inclusive democratic societies where people believe and feel that they have more in common than what divides them.

**One America Movement**—oneamericamovement.org/faith-communities/

The One America Movement is a national nonprofit confronting toxic polarization in society. It equips faith communities to confront division and work together across political, racial, and religious divides to solve problems.

**Soliya**—soliya.net

Founded in 2003 to use social circles in the digital space to change the world, Soliya teaches young adults to approach differences constructively and lead with empathy to thrive in an interconnected, pluralistic world.

**The Polarization and Social Change Lab at Stanford University**—www.pascl.stanford.edu

Rising political polarization and declining civility in political engagement are critical problems because they are barriers to addressing social problems. Without discussing the root causes of deep political divisions, it is nearly impossible to resolve pressing issues like global warming, poverty, immigration, and healthcare. This lab researches actionable solutions to reverse rising polarization and incivility in America. A multidisciplinary team theorizes interventions, evaluates them with data, pursues partnerships with organizations to directly intervene, and disseminates findings to political leaders and the general public.

**Sustained Dialogue Institute**—sustaineddialogue.org

Sustained Dialogue is an intentional, patented, and replicable peace process used to improve challenging relationships and come to action in intergroup conflicts. The Sustained Dialogue Institute helps people transform conflictual relationships and design change processes around the world. It defines dialogue as "listening deeply enough to be changed by what you learn."

**Weave: The Social Fabric Project, from the Aspen Institute**—weavers.org

Weave: The Social Fabric Project tackles the problem of broken social trust that leaves Americans divided, lonely, and in social gridlock. Weave connects, supports, and invests in local leaders stepping up to weave a new, inclusive social fabric where they live. The project was founded by *New York Times* columnist and author David Brooks at the Aspen Institute.

**AllSides Technologies Inc.**—www.allsides.com/about

AllSides Technologies Inc. strengthens America's democratic society with balanced news, media bias ratings, diverse perspectives, and real conversation. It aims to expose people to information and ideas from all sides of the political spectrum so they can better understand the world—and each other.

**American Press Institute**—americanpressinstitute.org/truth-telling-in-a-time-of-misinformation-and-polarization/

This report from the American Press Institute guides journalists in responding to rampant misinformation and learning how to parse fake news from legitimate items. It offers guidance for recognizing attempts at manipulation and staying clear when encountering a variety of sources. The report also advises when and how to report on false information and how journalists who may be attacked by vindictive leaders might respond. Finally, the materials address the very real issue of not expanding divides through reporting.

**American Listening Project**—american-listening-project.org

This site offers 15-minute sessions featuring Americans listening to one another across political divides.

**Civil Squared**—civilsquared.org/about/

Civil Squared aims to get people with different viewpoints talking in order to move toward creating the most effective solutions to communal challenges. It believes civil discourse is essential to building and maintaining a free and prosperous society. Its mission is to support the building of a free society by creating spaces for civil conversations among independent thinkers.

**The Fulcrum**—thefulcrum.us/about-us/our-mission

The Fulcrum is a platform where political insiders and outsiders are informed, meet, talk, and act to repair democracy. The Fulcrum is a project of and funded by the Bridge Alliance Education Fund. Founding funds came from the Hewlett Foundation, the Bridge Alliance Education Fund, Arnold Ventures, the Unite America Institute, the Gaia Fund, Craig Newmark Philanthropies, the Lizzie and Jonathan M. Tisch Foundation, and the Thornburg Foundation.

**The Flip Side**—www.theflipside.io

The Flip Side is on a mission to bridge the gap between liberals and conservatives. It offers smart, concise summaries of political analysis from conservative and liberal media. Its goal is to become a news source for liberals, moderates, independents, conservatives, and even the apolitical. The Flip Side distributes a free daily email offering the most thoughtful points from the left, right, and in between across 30-plus news sources.

### The Transpartisan Review—transpartisanreview.org

A. Lawrence Chickering and James S. Turner were cofounders of the Transpartisan Review. Chickering helped establish several public policy organizations, including the International Center for Economic Growth. He is the author of *Beyond Left and Right* and the coauthor with Turner of *Voice of the People: The Transpartisan Imperative in American Life*. Turner is a founding partner in the Washington, DC, law firm of Swankin & Turner. He has appeared before every major consumer regulatory agency, including the Food and Drug Administration, Environmental Protection Agency, Consumer Product Safety Commission, and Federal Trade Commission.

### Ballotpedia—ballotpedia.org/Main_Page

Ballotpedia is the digital encyclopedia of American politics and the nation's premier resource for unbiased information on elections, politics, and policy. It provides readers with curated content on US politics. Its team is firmly committed to neutrality in all content. Ballotpedia is a nonprofit with a mission to educate.

### Bipartisan Policy Center—bipartisanpolicy.org/about/

A nonprofit organization to ensure policymakers work across party lines to create bipartisan solutions. Since 2007, the Bipartisan Policy Center has helped shepherd countless bills through Congress.

### Commission on Civility and Effective Governance at the Center for the Study of the Presidency and Congress—www.thepresidency.org/commission-on-civility-effective-governance

This commission attempts to encourage American political leaders to generate innovative solutions for national challenges. This commission also seeks to include a wide array of leaders working together amid an increasingly compartmentalized federal government and to educate and inspire the next generation of America's leaders to incorporate civility, inclusiveness, and character into their public and private lives and discourse.

**Former Members of Congress**—www.usafmc.org

FMC is a nonprofit focused on Congress and involving former and current members of Congress on a bipartisan basis. More than 800 members participate in pro bono public service programs and initiatives. The organization also convenes congressional study groups every year as it seeks to strengthen Congress by creating across-the-aisle opportunities for legislators to work together. Additional efforts focus on educating the public about US representative democracy, public service, and Congress as an institution. Chartered by Congress since 1983, it is not funded by Congress. It is a 501(c)(3) tax-exempt nonprofit organization.

**The Institute for Civility**—www.instituteforcivility.org

Since 1997, the Institute for Civility has been promoting civility in government, workplaces, schools, and elsewhere. In 2023, it updated its name from the Institute for Civility in Government to better reflect the broad scope of its reach. This is a grassroots, nonpartisan nonprofit.

**Next Generation, a program of the National Institute for Civil Discourse**—nxtgenusa.org

Next Generation works directly with state legislators to address incivility and polarization at the state level. Next Generation offers an interactive, half-day workshop titled *Building Trust through Civil Discourse* that is designed and delivered *by* state legislators *for* state legislators.

**Unite America Institute**—www.uniteamericainstitute.org

The research and education arm of the voters first movement, United America seeks to understand the root causes of polarization in the US political system. It's a nonprofit 501(c)(3) organization encouraging broad-based, nonpartisan civic engagement and political participation that also engages in research and scholarly analysis on important issues of public concern, including the root causes, effects, and potential solutions to political polarization and partisanship.

**Bridging Divides Initiative at Princeton University**—bridgingdivides.princeton.edu

BDI is a nonpartisan research project that tracks and mitigates political violence in the United States.

**USC Center for the Political Future**—dornsife.usc.edu/center-for-political-future/

USC Center for the Political Future combines rigorous intellectual inquiry and teaching to advance civil dialogue and research that transcends partisan divisions and finds solutions to pressing societal challenges. Its events, programs, scholarships, and internships train students for careers in public service and lifetimes of civic engagement.

**The Project on Civic Dialogue at the American University**—www.american.edu/spa/civic-dialogue/index.cfm

Founded in 2018, the Project on Civic Dialogue fosters opportunities for active and worthwhile conversations. It operates from two core values: First, that dialogue is a skill that can be learned and must be practiced (and not a spectator sport). And second, that expressive freedom is a necessary condition for dialogue, but the real work is in collaborative inquiry, listening, and learning.

**American Public Square**—americanpublicsquare.org

A Kansas City–based community organization working to improve the tone and quality of public discourse by convening groups and creating space for respectful dialogue on important topics, educating community members about why engaging in this way is important and how to do it well, and engaging diverse segments of society to explore multiple perspectives.

**Millions of Conversations**—www.millionsofconversations.com

Headquartered in Nashville, this program developed a strategic theory of change that combines national media engagement with grassroots organizing to resolve conflict, heal divides, and strengthen democracy in America. Millions of Conversations exposes and counters currents of mis- and disinformation that can lead to fear, hate, and violence. It challenges narratives that stigmatize Americans, disrupts intolerance before it takes root, and helps heal communities so that all Americans can experience a sense of belonging.

## TED Talks

Peter Coleman: "Why We Are Stuck: The Attraction of a Polarized America"—www.youtube.com/watch?v=zdrdhU8WrfA

Joan Blades and John Gables: "Free Yourself from Your Filter Bubbles"—www.youtube.com/watch?v=jtVIDBs60S8

Jonathan Haidt: "The Moral Roots of Liberals and Conservatives"—www.ted.com/talks/jonathan_haidt_the_moral_roots_of_liberals_and_conservatives?language=en

Jonathan Haidt: "Can a Divided America Heal?"—www.ted.com/talks/jonathan_haidt_can_a_divided_america_heal?language=en

Robb Willer: "How to Have Better Political Conversations"—www.ted.com/talks/robb_willer_how_to_have_better_political_conversations?language=en

David Brooks and Gretchen Carlson: "Political Common Ground in a Polarized United States"—www.ted.com/talks/gretchen_carlson_david_brooks_political_common_ground_in_a_polarized_united_states?language=en

Yuval Noah Harari: "Nationalism vs. Globalism: The New Political Divide"—www.ted.com/talks/yuval_noah_harari_nationalism_vs_globalism_the_new_political_divide?language=en

Eve Pearlman: "How to Lead a Conversation between People Who Disagree"—www.ted.com/talks/eve_pearlman_how_to_lead_a_conversation_between_people_who_disagree?language=en

Arthur Brooks: "A Conservative Plea: Let's Work Together"—www.ted.com/talks/arthur_brooks_a_conservative_s_plea_let_s_work_together?language=en

Michael Sandel: "The Lost Art of Political Debate"—www.ted.com/talks/michael_sandel_the_lost_art_of_democratic_debate?language=en

Jonas Gahr Store: "In Defense of Dialogue"—www.ted.com/talks/jonas_gahr_store_in_defense_of_dialogue?language=en

Julia Galef: "Why You Think You're Right—Even If You're Wrong"—www.ted.com/talks/julia_galef_why_you_think_you_re_right_even_if_you_re_wrong?language=en

Pia Mancini: "How to Upgrade Democracy for the Internet Era"—www.ted.com/talks/pia_mancini_how_to_upgrade_democracy_for_the_internet_era?language=en

Jonathan Haidt: "How Common Threats Can Make Common (Political) Ground"—www.youtube.com/watch?v=v3o-F94S4FI

Celeste Headlee: "10 Ways to Have a Better Conversation"—www.youtube.com/watch?v=R1vskiVDwl4

Özlem Cekic: "Why I Have Coffee with People Who Send Me Hate Mail"—www.ted.com/talks/ozlem_cekic_why_i_have_coffee_with _people_who_send_me_hate_mail?language=en

Krista Tippett's interview of Derek Black and Matthew Stevenson: "Befriending Radical Disagreement"—onbeing.org/programs/derek -black-and-matthew-stevenson-befriending-radical-disagreement/

Krista Tippett's interview of Sally Kohn and Erick Erickson: "Relationship across Rupture, about Bridging Political Divides"—onbeing .org/programs/sally-kohn-and-erick-erickson-relationship-across -rupture-oct18/

# Letters from Civility Sponsors

"Delta Dental cares not only about what goes into your mouth, but also what comes out of it."

That tagline was irresistible. But initially, I couldn't figure out how to justify a corporate investment in the Civility Project when asked to sponsor what was just an idea in 2020.

We are a dental benefits company. Our mission is to improve oral health through benefit plans, advocacy, and community support.

What does civility have to do with any of that?

Everything.

Civility is essential to solving problems, growing business, influencing policy, and providing value. We simply cannot succeed at anything we need to do at our company if people are tearing each other apart.

No one can.

That realization and my decades-long personal and professional friendship with Nolan Finley and Stephen Henderson sealed the deal. Delta Dental was the singular sponsor of the Civility Project in the beginning. Now we are honored to be supporting "The Guide to Civility" along with Huntington Bank and the Ralph C. Wilson Foundation.

Nolan and Steve are unlikely friends, an odd couple of opposites whose chemistry is infectious and whose story is endearing. Their differences and repartee make a Sunday-morning talk show or a happy hour over a glass of bourbon feel a bit like a sporting event—with some fouls and time-outs.

But never any injuries.

They are so protective of their friendship and so determined to model civility for the community they love, they defend each other from those who would dare to attack. I've seen them do so countless times in low- and high-stakes situations.

They're effective because they took the time and did the work to know the content of one another's character and understand the origins of one another's beliefs. They really like each other, and their relationship seems buoyed by their differences.

Curiosity and vulnerability are key to the depth and the durability of their bond. They ask questions. They listen. They seek to understand, and they're willing to learn, to grow, and even to be wrong.

And they're passionate about using their experience, expertise, and influence to inspire a grassroots movement to counter the hate, ignorance, and fear mounting in our nation.

More than a tagline or a good business move, I believe Delta Dental has invested in a lifeline for our company, our community, and ultimately, our democracy.

*Margaret Trimer*
Vice President of Strategic Partnerships
Delta Dental of Michigan, Ohio, and Indiana

Dear Friends of the Civility Project,

The revered and brilliant Talmudic thinker and scholar Hillel the Elder encapsulated the foundational principle for all generations to strive for: "Love your neighbor as yourself and let civility guide all your interactions with others."

These words create both an obligation and an imperative that, when adhered to, can guide individuals and societies to find common ground even where significant differences and disagreements are evident.

This is in fact what attracted us to the work of the Civility Project. The notion that Nolan Finley and Steve Henderson, adherents to two very diverse and different political ideologies, could respectfully discuss and debate without acrimony was extremely refreshing and uplifting. The civility they advocate and the harmony they display underscore the capacity for individuals to differ on issues while still remaining amiable, courteous, and considerate.

As we observe the world and times we live in, it is especially critical that each of us, no matter our station in life or personal proclivities, find ways to fulfill and promote Hillel's ideal for a just and civil society.

We are grateful to Nolan and Steve for modeling these essential values, to Margaret Trimer and Delta Dental for their partnership in this worthwhile endeavor, and to Lynne Golodner for her leadership and direction.

With best wishes for continued success and blessings to all who undertake and promote civility,

All the best,

*Gary Torgow*
Chairman, Huntington Bank

Eugene Driker was a prominent attorney in Southeast Michigan, a Life Trustee of the Ralph C. Wilson, Jr., Foundation, and a mentor. He passed away in the fall of 2022. Eugene was deeply troubled by the growing lack of civility within the communities that we live and the democratic republic writ large. Even though the foundation does not fund advancing democracy causes, Eugene would often question if the foundation could fund anything that could help improve the situation.

When I learned of the intent of Stephen Henderson, Nolan Finley, and Lynne Golodner to write the essays that would become *The Civility Book*, I was quick to offer support from a discretionary fund in order to honor Eugene, his love of country, and his commitment to community.

The apparent lack of civility in today's society has many of us searching to understand the future of our country, our communities, and our personal and professional relationships. I once sought out healthy, spirited debate and sharing of differing opinions with people I respected. Only occasionally did these exchanges substantially alter my beliefs; however, they almost always made me more aware, increased my understanding, and led to common understanding among the participants about what issues or topics could or should be addressed. Today, I hesitate before entering into such discussions out of fear of an extreme reaction and/or the potential of damaging relationships.

It seems as if political beliefs have replaced facts. Many sit in engineered media echo chambers, hardening opinion instead of seeking to understand the position of others. In numerous cases, where there once was healthy debate that led to common direction, there is now anger that leads to greater division. It's no surprise that anxiety and depression are increasing at unprecedented levels. There has never been a better time to explore civility's role in our lives.

Why be civil? Because our country, our communities, and our own personal health depend on it. Eugene would be proud to see the foundation supporting this book. He would be optimistic that all who read it will be moved to reverse the incivility that is blanketing our nation, one relationship at a time.

Sincerely,

*David O. Egner*
President & CEO
Ralph C. Wilson, Jr., Foundation

# About the Authors

**Nolan Finley** has held many positions at *The Detroit News* since the start of his career there as a copyboy, including city editor, business editor, politics editor, and deputy managing editor. In 2000, he was named editorial page editor, a position from which he directs the expression of the newspaper's editorial position on various national and local issues and writes a column in the Sunday newspaper. He graduated from Schoolcraft College and Wayne State University, and in 2012 he was inducted into the Michigan Journalism Hall of Fame. Finley is also cohost of *One Detroit* on Detroit Public Television.

**Stephen Henderson** is an American journalist and winner of the 2014 Pulitzer Prize for Commentary and the 2014 National Association of Black Journalists Journalist of the Year Award—both received while writing for the *Detroit Free Press*. A native of Detroit, Henderson is a graduate of the University of Detroit Jesuit High School and the University of Michigan. In 2020 he founded *BridgeDetroit*, where he serves as executive editor. Henderson is cohost of *One Detroit* and host of *American Black Journal* on Detroit Public Television.

**Lynne Golodner** is a native of Detroit and an award-winning author, marketing entrepreneur, and writing coach. Her writing has appeared in *45th Parallel*, the *Chicago Tribune*, *Better Homes and Gardens*, *Midwest Living*, and many more publications. She served as executive director of the Civility Project from 2020–24. Golodner teaches writing around the world, leads writers' retreats, and has taught writing at University of Detroit Mercy since 2010 and with WritingWorkshops.com since 2018. A former Fulbright Specialist, Golodner is a graduate of the University of Michigan and Goddard College and earned a certificate in entrepreneurship from the Goldman Sachs 10,000 Small Businesses program at Wayne State University.